CRAWLEY · MID-SUSSEX
EAST GRINSTEAD · HAYWARDS HEATH ·

C000130205

4
Ho
Charlwood 6 7
Gat
8
Co
Ifield 10 11
Three Bridges 12 13
Crabbet Park
CRAWLEY
22
18 Crawley Down 19
20 East Grinstead 21
22 Ashurst Wood
Bewbush 14 Tilgate 15
Furnace Green 16 17

34 35
Broadbridge Heath 38
Horsham
36 37

17 Balcombe

Cuckfield 23
24 25
Haywards Heath
26 27

Burgess Hill 28 29

Hurstpierpoint 30 31
Hassocks 32 33 Ditchling

Scale of street plans: 4 Inches to 1 Mile (unless otherwise stated)

Motorway

'A' Road / Dual

'B' Road / Dual

Minor Road / Dual

Track

Pedestrianized

Railway / Station

Footpath

Every effort has been made to verify the accuracy of information in this book but the publishers cannot accept responsibility for expense or loss caused by an error or omission. Information that will be of assistance to the user of the maps will be welcomed.

The representation on these maps of a road, track or path is no evidence of the existence of a right of way.

Stream / River

Canal

One-way Street

P Car Park

C Public Convenience

i Tourist Information

+ Place of Worship

● Post Office

Street plans prepared and published by ESTATE PUBLICATIONS, Bridewell House, TENTERDEN, KENT. The Publishers acknowledge the co-operation of the local authorities of towns represented in this atlas.

Ordnance Survey® This product includes mapping data licensed from Ordnance Survey® with the permission of the Controller of Her Majesty's Stationery Office.

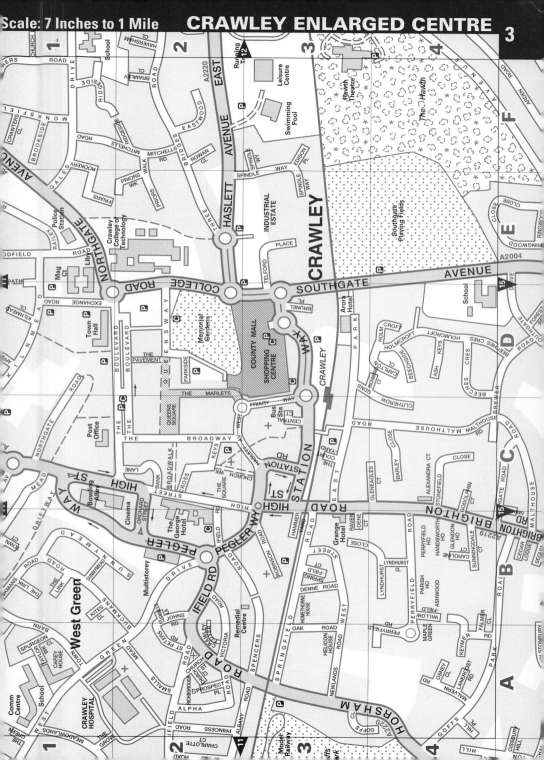

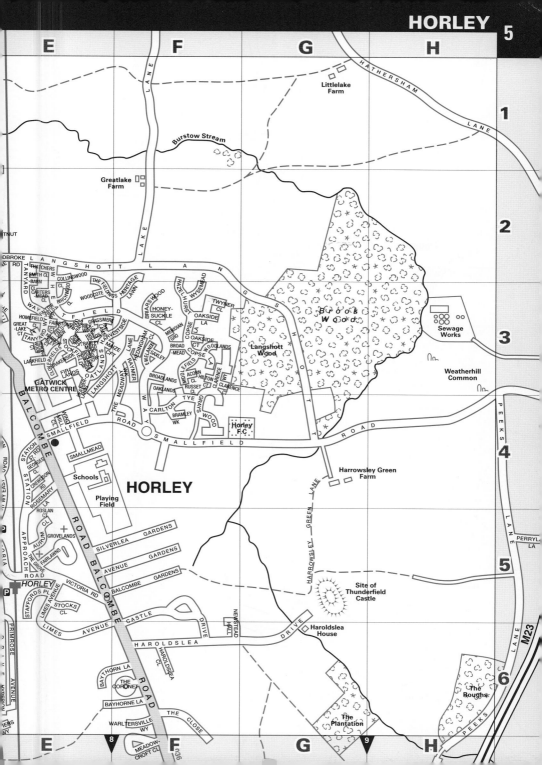

E F G H

1

Littlelake
Farm

HATHERSHAM

LANE

Burstow Stream

2

Greatlake
Farm

TNUT

LANGSHOTT LANE

DBROKE
RD
THATCHERS
TANYARD
SMITH CL
BARN
CARTERS
MEAD
CL
BROCKWOOD
COLLINGWOOD
THE FIELDINGS
WOODCOTE CL
HERITAGE
LAWN
BRIARSWOOD
HAZELHURST
WYSEMEAD
TWYNER
CL
HONEY-
SUCKLE
CL
OAKSIDE
Brook
Wood
WAY
GREAT
LAKE
CL
HOMEFIELD
FAIRSTONES
GRASSMERE
MERIDIAN
GRO
OAKSIDE
CT
WOODLANDS
Sewage
Works
TANYA
FIELD
SHAKESPEARE
RABBIT
CL
HEDINGHAM
WEALDEN
CL
BROAD
MEAD
SAXLEY
COPSE
CT
CL
3
LARKFIELD
FIRLANDS
LANE
RAYMER
MAIZE
ACORN
CL
HILTON
CL
CLARENCE
WY
Langshott
Wood
GATWICK
METRO CENTRE
OATLANDS
LANGSHOTT
THE MEADOW
BROADLANDS
RUSSET
CL
CLARENCE
Weatherhill
Common
WINDMILL
CL
CARLTON
TYE
GRAYS
WOOD
BRAMLEY
WK
SMALLFIELD
Horley
F.C.
ROAD
WAY
SMALLFIELD
ROAD
4
SMALLMEAD
STATION
ST RD
GEORGES
RD
Schools
Harrowsley Green
Farm
PEEKS
CREWLSON
RD
ROSEMARY
LA
HORLEY
ROSLAN
CL
Playing
Field
BALCOMBE
LANE
AUCK
GROVELANDS
PERRYL.
LA
THE GROVE
FAIRLAWNS
SILVERLEA
GARDENS
5
HORLEY
STAFFORDS PL
AVENUE
GARDENS
Site of
Thunderfield
Castle
P
VICTORIA RD
ROAD
BALCOMBE
STOCKS
CL
BALCOMBE
GARDENS
HARROWSLEY GREEN LANE
DRIVE
LIMES AVENUE
CASTLE
NEWSTEAD
HALL
Haroldslea
House
DRIVE
PRIMROSE
APPROACH ROAD
HAROLDSLEA
HAROLDSLEA
CL
M23
BAYTHORN LA
THE
CORONET
DRIVE
ROAD
THE
Roughs
6
AVENUE
BAYHORNE LA
WARLTERSVILLE
WY
THE
CLOSE
The
Plantation
PEEKS

E F G H
8 9
MEADOW-
CROFT CL

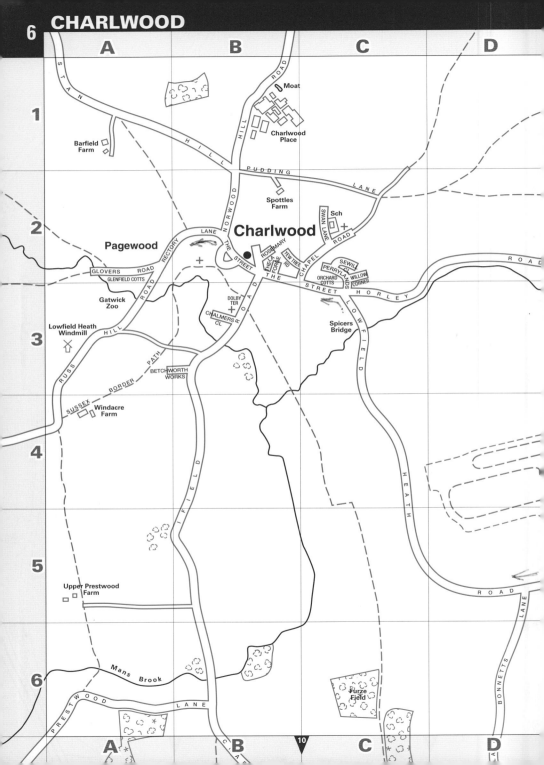

A   B   C   D

1

Moat

Barfield
Farm

Charlwood
Place

HILL ROAD

STAN

HILL

NORWOOD

PUDDING   LANE

SWAN LANE

Spottles
Farm

Sch

2

Pagewood

Charlwood

RECTORY   LANE

THE STREET

ROSEMARY

THE
FORGE
LA

NEW TREE

CHAPEL RD

SEWILL CL

PERRYLANDS

WILLOW CORNER

ROAD

GLOVERS   ROAD

GLENFIELD COTTS

ORCHARD
COTTS

Gatwick
Zoo

THE   STREET

HORLEY

ROAD

DOLBY
TER

CHALMERS
CL

Spicers
Bridge

LOWFIELD

Lowfield Heath
Windmill

HILL

3

RUSS

PATH

BETCHWORTH
WORKS

BORDER

SUSSEX

Windacre
Farm

IFIELD   ROAD

HEATH

4

5

Upper Prestwood
Farm

ROAD

LANE

BONNETTS

6

Mans   Brook

Furze
Field

PRESTWOOD   LANE

A   B   C   D

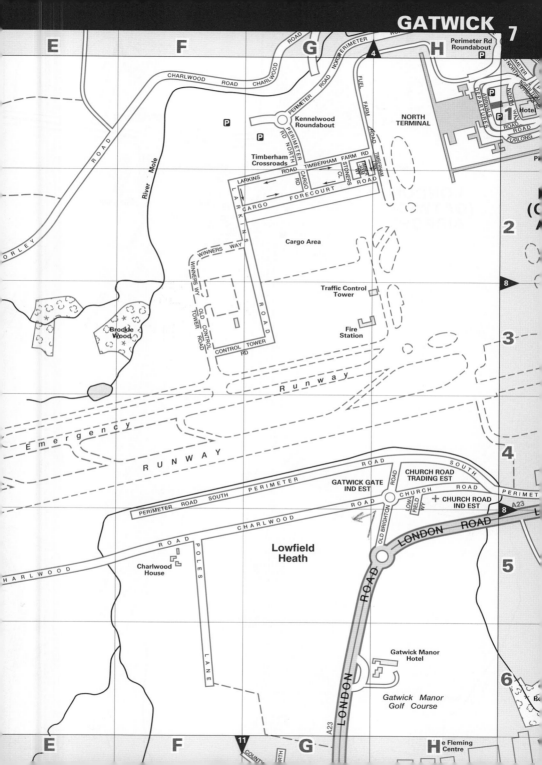

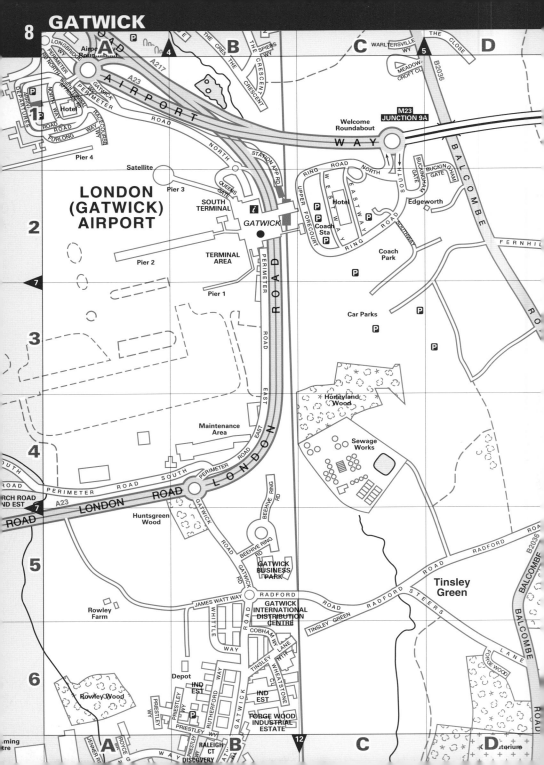

E ▲5 F G H

Plan ?

M23

M23 JUNCTION 9

Bellhatch Wood

BROADBRIDGE

Bridges Wood

CHURCH ROAD LANE

DONKEY LANE

ROAD PEEKS CHURCH LANE

School

Fernhill

PEEKS LANE

CHURCH LANE

GREEN LANE

Burstow

+

Keep
Corr

B2037 LANE

M23

Burstow Hall

ANTLANDS LANE

ANTLANDS LA WEST

ANTLANDS LANE EAST

Shipley Bridge

Shipley Bridge

ANTLANDS LANE

B2037

ROAD

Kiln Heath

ROAD

B2037

LCOMBE ROAD

BRIDGE LANE

SHIPLEY LANE

Burstow Farm

Wellfield Copse

Heathy Ground

Rec Grnd

BANK

ST FRANCIS

BORERS 22

KNOWLE

ELGER
WY ROFEYS CL

CHURCH RD

COPTHORNE LANE

SHIPLEY BRIDGE LANE

Sch

THE GLEBE

CHURCH ROAD

BEECHEY CL

BEECHEY WAY

OAK CLOSE

DAWN
RISE

BROOKSIDE

WESTWAY

MEADOW RD

THE MEADOW

THE
MEADOW
GREEN

THE MEADOW

NEW TOWN ROAD

KNOWLE CL

PINETREES

Copt

BROOKHILL

BRIDGELANDS WAY

ERICA CL

SMEAD ROAD

BROOK
VIEW

AKEHURST CL

CHURCH LANE

Sch

FAIRWAY

P

New Town

COPT

ERICA CL

DRIVE

ROAD

URCH LANE

BRACKEN

COMMON RD

COPTHORNE

THE GABLES

E F 13 G H COPTH

1 2 3 4 5 6

A full-page street map of Ifield, with grid references A–D across the top and 1–6 down the left side.

Labels visible on the map include:

Grid A:
- Pockneys Farm
- Furlong Farm
- Ifield Golf Course
- Club
- River Mole

Grid B:
- CHARLWOOD (ROAD)
- Ifield Wood
- Cophall Wood
- Ifield Court Farm
- Ifield Court Hotel
- Moat
- IFIELD (ROAD)
- RUSPER (ROAD)
- Mill Stream
- Playing Field
- WHITEHALL DR
- MERLIN
- LANCELOT
- GALAHAD RD
- EXCALIBUR
- GUINEVERE
- ARTHUR RD
- CAMELOT
- STANBRIDGE
- CAPSEY WAY
- MIDDLETON RD
- GORLING
- HANBURY
- DEWAR RD
- STRICKLAND
- THE MILLBANK
- SHARPTHORNE CL
- PEVEREL RD
- POYNINGS ROAD
- DEVEREL DRIVE
- MAINFIELD CL
- BITMEAD
- DEALL
- HYDE
- LAWS
- THE MILLBANK
- CAM

Grid C:
- Ifield Hall
- IFIELD ROAD
- BONNETTS (LA)
- Strafford Bridge
- RIVER MEAD
- STRATHMORE RD
- Ifield Green
- TWEED LA
- RECTORY LA
- MILL LA
- Cricket Ground
- School
- RUSPER ROAD
- RECTORY ST
- LOWFIELD
- PARHAM RD
- LAVINGTON CL
- CUSTOM
- LANDING
- LINCHMERE PL
- WARREN
- PATCHING ROAD
- RUSPERS KEEP
- ALDBOROUGH
- LADY MARGARET RD
- SELHAM CL
- SHIPLEY ROAD
- SLINFOLD WK
- SHIPLEY RD
- SOUTHWATER CL
- COOLHAM
- RUDGWICK RD
- TANGMERE RD
- TREYFORD CL
- OVERDENE DRIVE
- IFIELD
- Ifield Park
- HILLMEAD
- PARKFIELD CL
- HIGHAMS HILL
- CRESCENT
- HIGHAMS
- WINDY RIDGE
- GOSSOPS GRN
- CHERWELL
- RUTHER
- AVON WK
- DERWENT
- CUCKMERE
- KENNET
- MEDWAY RD
- Comm Centre
- CAPEL LANE
- Sch
- Playing Field
- School
- Ifield
- School
- DEERSWOOD CT
- NUTHURST
- ALBERT CT
- FRISTON WK

Grid D:
- The Brook
- Club
- Crawley R.F.C.
- IFIELD
- STRAFFORD AVE
- LANGLEY
- KIRKFORD CL
- HARD
- OLD MANOR CL
- Sch
- GREEN DRIVE
- FRISTON
- ALBERT CT
- DRIVE
- COB CRESCENT WK
- FILBERT DRIVE
- ELMWOOD LA
- NURSERLANDS
- CRAIGANS
- OAKLANDS
- RYELANDS
- DOWER WK
- DAIRY FIELDS
- POLLARDS
- OATLANDS
- HASCOMBE CT
- DUNSFOLD
- PADDOCKHURST ROAD
- KIDBI
- MAANS

Grid A (bottom):
- HOYLAKE
- MOOR PARK CRES
- ST ANDREWS RD
- PRESTWICK
- BIRKDALE
- MUIRFIELD
- PUFFIN
- DOBBINS
- BITTERN
- FAIRWAY
- STACKFIELD RD

Column letters repeated at bottom: A B 14 C D

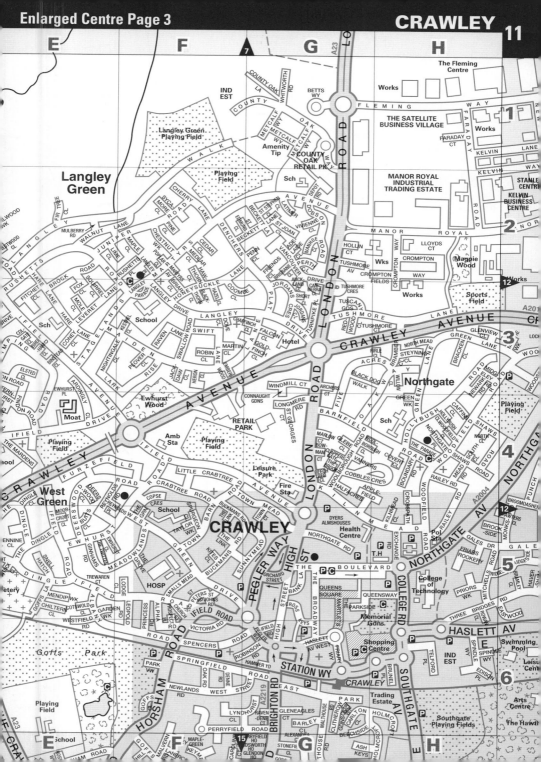

E F 9 G H

M23 JUNCTION 10

COPTHORNE WAY

COPTHORNE COMMON RD

COPT

1

Copthorne Golf Course

Copthorne Common

A264

Hotel

Kits Bridge

HOLLOW ROAD

Pot Common

22

Heathyground Wood

Coombes Wood

2

Marsh Wood

Copthorne Wood

Dixons Heath

Drivers Wood

OLD HOLLOW ROAD

3

Crabbet Park

Equitation Centre

Gatwick Worth Hotel

Crabbet Park

4

Burley Wood

M23

Brewhouse Wood

Horsepasture Wood

Layhouse Wood

SEDGEFIELD

LINGFIELD DR

KELSO

CLOSE

HEXHAM CLOSE

HILL

ROAD

TURNERS

HILL

ROAD

5

TAUNTON

LEICESTER

THE RIDINGS

SALEHURST ROAD

TICEHURST

TURNERS HILL

ROAD

WALLACE LA

Compasses Corner

HAROLD RD

Worth Lodge Farm

Fourteen Acre Rough

6

Worth

WORTH WAY

Oaken Wood

The Burches

BALCOMBE

E F 17 G H

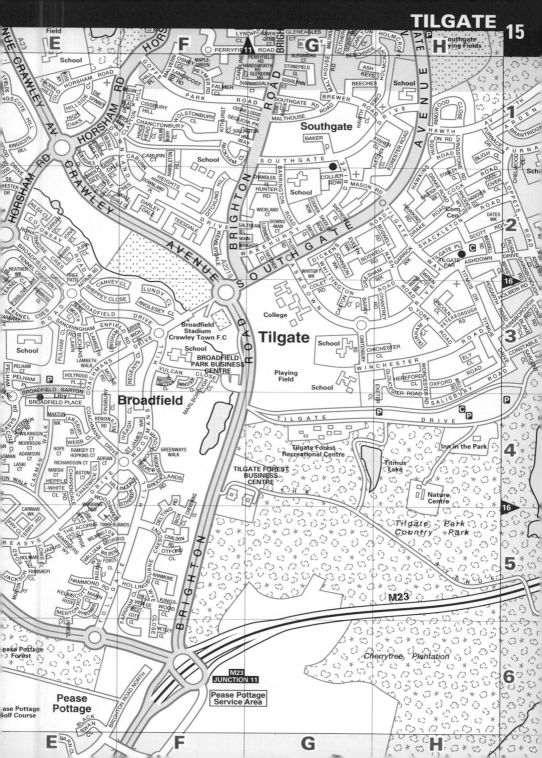

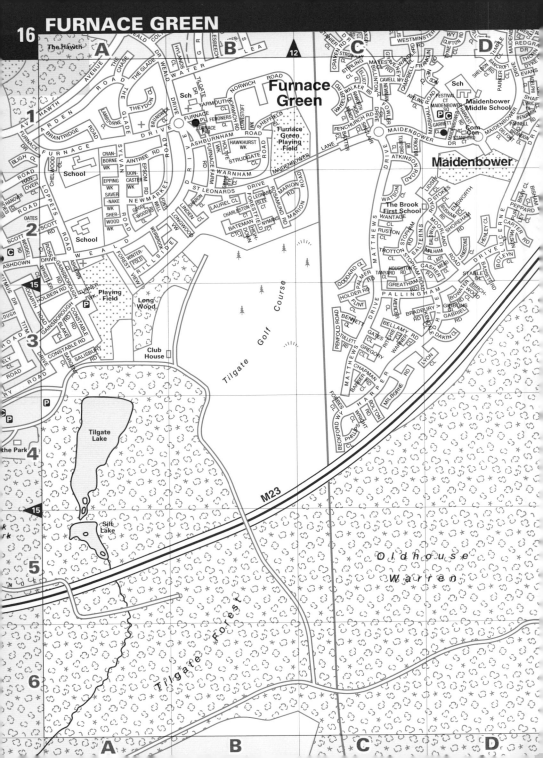

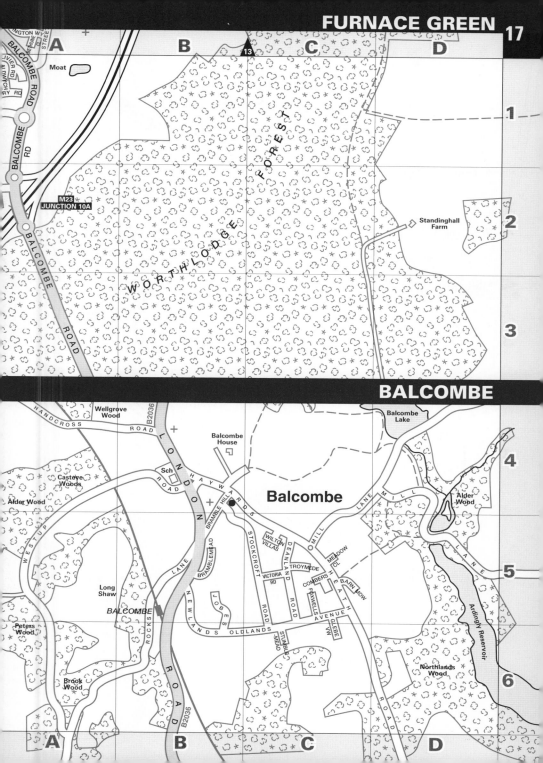

A   B   C   D

Moat

BALCOMBE ROAD

ETHUNE WY
STREET
TIER RD
DYWCH
RY RD
NGTON W

1

2

M23
JUNCTION 10A

W O R T H L O D G E   F O R E S T

BALCOMBE ROAD

Standinghall
Farm

3

HANDCROSS ROAD

Wellgrove
Wood

B2036

LONDON

Balcombe
House

Balcombe
Lake

4

Casteye
Woods

Sch

HAYWARDS

Balcombe

MILL LANE

Alder
Wood

Alder Wood

BRAMBLE HILL

WILTON
VILLAS

DEANLAND

MEADOW
CL

BARN MDW

5

WESTUP

ROAD

LANE

BRAMBLEMEAD

STOCKCROFT

VICTORIA
RD

TROYMEDE

ROAD

COMBERS
HEATH

GLEBE
VW

Long
Shaw

JOBES

FOXWELLS AVENUE

Ardingly Reservoir

BALCOMBE

ROCKS

NEWLANDS

OLDLANDS

ROAD

STUMBLE
MEAD

Northlands
Wood

Peters
Wood

6

Brook
Wood

ROAD

B2036

A   B   C   D

Felbridge

COPTHORNE

MILL LANE

TANGLE OAK LANE

EASTBOURNE ROAD

A22

THE LIMES

THE GLEBE

ARKENDALE

A264

ROAD

Cricket Grou

TWITTEN LA

TITHE ORCHARD

Hall

Sch

MOUNTER CL

EVELYN CL

WARREN CL

ROWPLATT

WHEELERS WY

ROAD

CRAWLEY

DOWN

ROAD

FELBRIDGE CT

STANDEN CL

THE MOORINGS

THE FELD

FELWATER CT

STREAM PK

A22

Ho

FURZE

L

IMBERH

THE FELBRIDGE CENTRE

BIRCHES INDUSTRIAL ESTATE

20

INDEPENDENT BUSINESS PARK

berhor School

NACE FARM ROAD

FELBRIDGE

HILL

ROAD

HOPHURST

The Birches

Play Fie

Felbridge Water

Greenfield Shaw

Imberhorne Farm

4

THE MARTINS

AW

20

Railway Shaw

5

BERHO

Great Wood

Rushetts Wood

Co

6

IMBERHORNE

Crocks Wo

E F G H

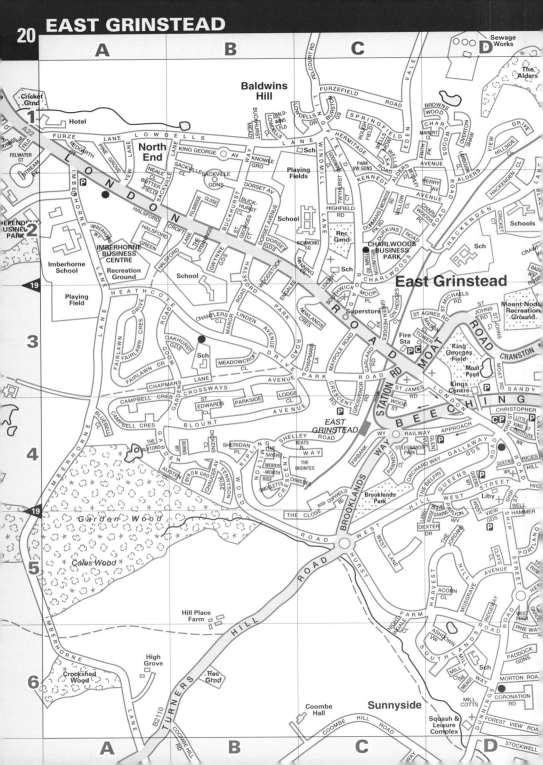

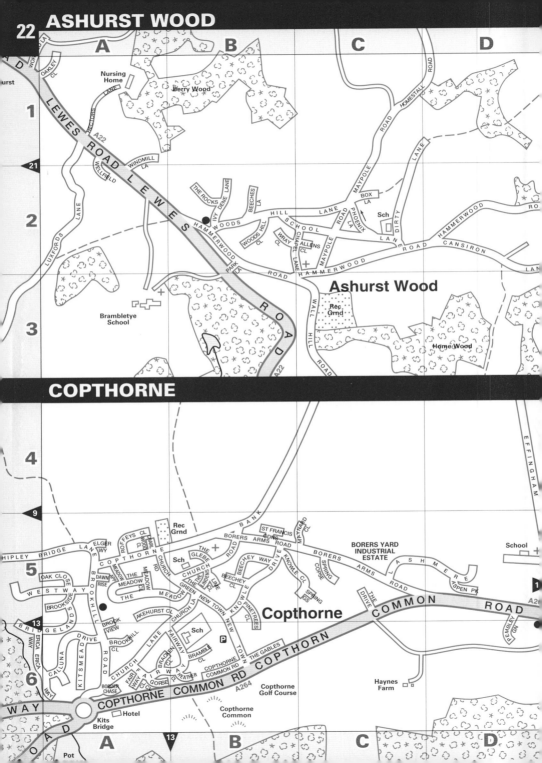

A **B** **C** **D**

1

Nursing Home

Berry Wood

LEWES ROAD

A22

21

WINDMILL LA

WELLFIELD

LEWES

2

THE ROCKS

IVY DENE LANE

BEECHES

WOODS HILL

WOODS CL

WRAY CL

ALLENS

CHAPEL LANE

MAYPOLE

HAMMERWOOD

PARK ROAD

HAMMERWOOD ROAD

HILL LANE

SCHOOL

MAYPOLE ROAD

PHOENIX LA

BOX LA

Sch

DIRTY LANE

HAMMERWOOD ROAD

CANSIRON LANE

RO

LUXFORDS LANE

Ashurst Wood

Brambletye School

Rec Grnd

WALL HILL ROAD

Home Wood

3

HOMESTALL ROAD

4

EFFINGHAM

9

HIPLEY BRIDGE LANE

ELGER WY

ROFFEYS CL

CHARL WOOD

Rec Grnd

BANK

ST FRANCIS GDNS

BORERS ARMS ROAD

MAYNARD CL

BORERS YARD INDUSTRIAL ESTATE

School

5

OAK CLOSE

WESTWAY

DAWNS RISE

BROOKHILL

COPTHORNE RD

THE MEADOW

CHURCH RD

THE GLEBE

Sch

CHURCH LINE

THE LINDENS

BEECHEY WAY

KNOWLE CL

DRIVE

BORERS COPSE

SPRING

ARMS ROAD

LASHMERE

OPEN PK

A2

1

BROOKSIDE

THE MEADOW

GREEN NEW TOWN LA

PINETREES

SPRING CL

Copthorne

THE DRIVE

COMMON ROAD

A26

13

ERICA WAY

ERICA

BRIDGE WAY

GELANDS DRIVE

BROOK VIEW

AKEHURST CL

BROOKHILL CL

CHURCH LA

FAIRWAY

NEW TOWN LA

KNOWLE

Sch

BRACKEN

P

BRAMBLE CL

THE GABLES

COMMON RD

COMMON RD

COPTHORN

PEMBLEY GN

6

KITSMEAD ROAD

CHURCH ROAD

BORDER CHASE

CALUNA WAY

FAIR WAY

GORSE

HEATHER

COPTHORNE COMMON RD

A264

Copthorne Golf Course

Haynes Farm

WAY

Kits Bridge

Hotel

Copthorne Common

Pot

A **B** **13** **C** **D**

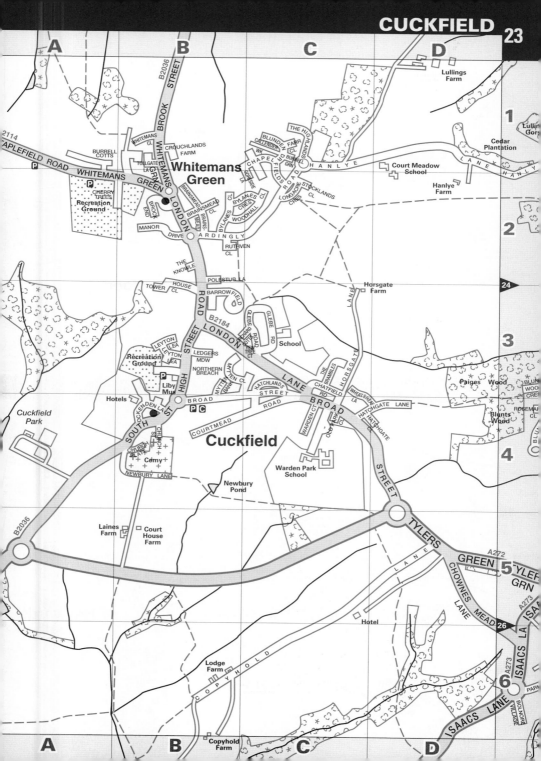

Whitemans Green

Cuckfield

A full-page street map of Haywards Heath.

Grid references: A, B, C, D (columns); 1, 2, 3, 4, 5, 6 (rows).

Borde Hill, Copyhold Bridge, Copyhold Lane, Wickham Wood, Sandridge La, Sugworth Farm, Sugworth Wood, Staves Copse, Haywards Heath Golf Course, The Drive, Club Ho, Roundwood Lane, Flat Wood, Borde Lane, Bitchen Wood, Beech, Portsmouth Wood, Spring Copse, Lutlings Gorse, Brook Lane, Gatesmead, High, Cedar Plantation, Hanlye Lane, 23, Balcombe, Penland, Birchen Lane, Sunte, Penland Farm, The Shinneins, Orchard Way, Fairfield, Oakhurst, Old Wickham La, Gander Grn, Oak La, Tavistock Summer School, Hill, Balcombe Road, Barn Mead, Cedars, Wickham Road, Summerhill Grange, B2028, Sports Ground, Harlands School, Penland Wood, Mill Green, Wickham Close, College Road, Gander Cl, Summerhill Cl, Sunte, Bridge, Turners Mill Cl, Bridgers, Burrell, Bridge Road Business Park, Gordon Road, Queens, West Common, Harlands Cl, Haywards Heath College, The Ashdown, Supermarket, Fire Sta, Amb Sta, Paiges Wood, Quarry Hill, Blunts Wood Cres, Harlands Road, Pasture Hill Road, Turners Mill, Bannister Wy, Great Heathmead, Market Place, Commercial Sq, Sydney Road, Church Road, Queens Road, Uttafield Ct, Rosemary Cl, Hillside Wk, The Droveway, The Dell, Blunts Wood, The Dolphin Leisure Centre, Winnals, Pk, Milton Ct, HAYWARDS HEATH, Clevelands, Clair Rd, Cricket Ground, The Heath Community Centre & Theatre, Oathall, St Pauls R.C. School, Lincoln, Lucastes, Heatherbank, Avenue, Courtos Av, Grange, 1.Byron Ct, 2.Chaucer Ct, 3.Kipling Ct, 4.Shelley Ct, 5.Tennyson Ct, 6.Milton Ct, Bodiam Cl, Clair Cl, The Heath Recreation Ground, Avenue, St Pauls, Farlington, Foxwarren Cl, Badger Dr, Sherwood Dr, Lucas Road, The Laurels, Nursery Cl, Wichperry Rd, Oaklands, Hudson Road, Newton Ct, Jireh, Gladepoint, Heath, Arbor Cl, Haywards Heath, Fairford, High Trees, Bents Wood, Warren Road, Chillis Wood, Paddockhall, Sergison Rd, Liby, Council Offices, T.H., Winkfield Ct, Ormerod, Health Centre, Trevelan, Ashurst, Haywarth School, Fairford, Mayflower Cl, Woodlands Rd, HAYWARDS HEATH HOSPITAL, The Bower, Brunswick Cl, Muster Green, North Road, Chelsea Arc, Highland, Clover, Hazel Grove, New, Maytower Cl, Fields End, Pinehurst Copse, TYLERS GRN, Isaacs La, A273, BUTLERS GREEN, RD, Playing Fields, Beech Hurst Recreation Ground, Pol Sta & Mag Court, Beech Hurst Cl, Wealden, MUSTER GREEN STH, Church Road, The Broadway, South Road, St Wilfrids Way, St Josephs, The Orchards, Augustine Way, Sch, Bluebell Cl, Priory, Rother Cl, Downes Mead, Lane, Bolnore, Hanover Cl, Amber, A272, A272, Bramber, Victoria Park Recreation Ground, 26, Green Lane

A B C D

REEDS LANE

BRIGHTON ROAD

B2118

A23

LANE

1

Coombe
Farm

Coombe
Wood

B2116

HENFIELD

2

West
Town
Farm

KEMPS

WESTERN WAY

West House
Farm

HOLDERS

ROAD

BRIGHTON

ALBOURNE

B2116

West
Town

ORCHARD WAY

WESTERN RD

HUNTERS
MEAD

THE BARN

CL

Hall

School

Albourne
Green

HUNTERS
MEAD

BARLEY
CROFT

Pakyns
Manor House

Hurstpierpoint

ROAD

High

STREET

THE
TWITTEN

3

STANLEYS

LEYFIELD

Willow
Copse

CHURCH

LANE

WELLCROFT
COTTS

CHURCH LANE

Cricket
Ground

Grange
Farm

Washbrooks
Farm

BULLFINCH LANE

Albourne
Street

4

Cutlers Brook

Wanbarrow
Farm

5

Alder
Shaw

ROAD

B2117

B2118

Randolph
Farm

6

Jammeson
Farm

Stalkers
Copse

BRIGHTON

A23

A B C D

Rec Ground, WILLOW WAY, WILLOW, WILLOW GDNS, CHALKERS, CHALKERS LANE, DANWAY LA, Playing Field, Playing Field, Playing Field, Playing Field, St Johns College, Sandfield Shaw, CUCKFIELD ROAD, WESTERN RD, SERV RD, Rec Ground, IDEN, HURST, WHITES CL, BISHOPS CL, HANNINGT, Tilleys Copse, St LAWRENCE WAY, CRES, FAIRFIELD, The Wilderness, CHESTNUT GRO, WILDERNESS RD, MARCHANTS, ST CHRIS, TOWERS, St TOWERS PL, SUNWORTH, PARK, Village Centre, Liby, MANOR PL, NOR RD, Pol Sta, Sch, TRINITY, THE GLEBE, Health Centre, Ribbetts House, BROWN, TWINS RD, TRINITY CT, ROAD, HIGH ROAD, B2117, HIGH STREET, HASSOCKS ROAD, NEW FURLONG, PITT LANE, W FURLONG LA, GLEBE, Rec Grnd, SOUTH AVENUE, PARKVIEW, DOWNSVIEW, ABBERTON FIELD, HAILSHAMS, ST GEORGES PL, ST GEORGES LA, St GEORGES PL, CHERINGTON CL, PINE TREE, HIGHFIELD, SPINNEY, WICKHAM CLOSE, WICKHAM DR, DRIVE, COLLEGE, COLLEGE LANE, COLLEGE PL, Hurst Wickham, HURST WICKHAM CL, Golf Course, Reed Pond Shaw, PAVIL, Rec Ground, TOTT HILL, LYNTON CL, WOLSTONBURY CL, LYNTON CL, RANDIDDLES CL, WICKHAM HILL, ROAD, B2116, Cemy, Playing Field, BELMONT LANE, The Crossways, HAM, HAM Shaw, The Plantation, WAY, Stonecroft Copse, Danny Lake, Old Wood, Stonepound Crossroads, HURST RD, HURST ROAD, THE, B2116, LONDON ROAD, BRIGHTON ROAD, KEYMER, PINE TREES, STANFORD, STONEPOUND, NORTH, SOUTH, BANK, TIMOTHY, POUND GATE, 28, 32

Grid references: E, F, G, H across; 1, 2, 3, 4, 5, 6 down.

E   F   G   H

1

2

3

4

5

6

Castle Copse

Moated House Farm

Owlcastle Farm

Ibrook Park

(NORTH) HORSHAM BY-PASS (NORTH)

Dutchells Copse Pavilion

Motte & Bailey

CRAWLEY ROAD

A264

B2195

The Birches

Old Crawley Road

NEW MOORHEAD DR

KINGS MEAD

The Larches

EARLES MEADOW

CHERRY TREE WK

Sch

The Pines

WOOD END

ROWAN WAY

SYCAMORE AV

Littlehaven

LITTLEHAVEN

Lower Barn

Roffey

Playing Field

Cricket Grnd

Sch

Cemy

Little Haven

Parsonage Business Park

School

Comm Cent

Sports Grnd

School

Leechpool Wood

St Leonards

IND EST

Park Wood

Harwood Road

B2195 HARWOOD RD

HARWOOD ROAD

St. Leonards Park

Forest

School

37

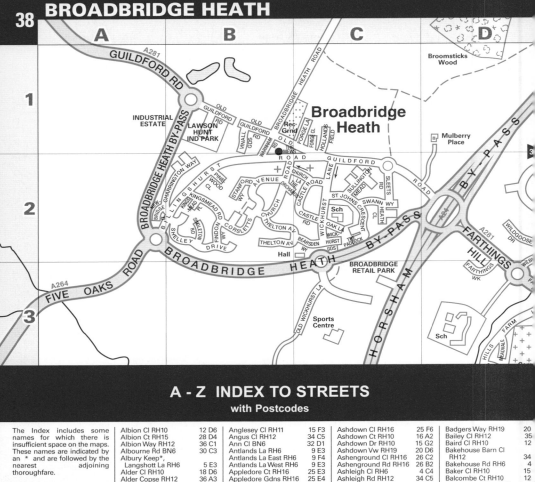

A - Z INDEX TO STREETS
with Postcodes

39

Newlands Rd,
Crawley RH11 3 A3
Newlands Rd,
Horsham RH12 34 C5
Newman Cl RH10 16 C1
Newmarket Rd RH10 16 A2
Newport Rd RH15 28 C3
Newstead Hall RH6 5 F5
Newton Cl RH16 25 F3
Newton Cl RH16 24 C5
Newton Rd,
Crawley RH10 12 A1
Newton Rd,
Haywards Heath RH16 25 F3
Nightingale Cl,
Crawley RH11 11 E3
Nightingale Cl,
East Grinstead RH19 20 C6
Nightingale Ind Est
RH12 34 D6
Nightingale La RH15 28 D6
Nightingale Rd RH12 34 D6
Nightingales Cl RH13 37 G1
Ninfield Cl RH11 14 C3
Niven Cl RH10 13 E6
Noahs Ark La RH15 25 F4
Noel Grn RH15 29 E2
Noel Rise RH15 29 E3
Norfolk Cl,
Crawley RH11 14 B3
Norfolk Cl, Horley RH6 4 C5
Norfolk Cl RH12 35 H4
Norfolk Ter RH11 37 E1
Norman Rd RH15 28 D4
Normandy RH12 36 D2
Normandy Cl,
Crawley RH10 16 C1
Normandy Cl,
East Grinstead RH19 21 E5
Normandy Gdns RH12 36 D2
Normanhurst Rd RH10 12 A5
North Bank BN6 32 A2
North Cl RH10 11 H4
North Cl BN6 32 A2
North End RH6 33 F3
North Heath Cl RH12 34 D4
North Heath Ind Est
RH12 34 D3
North heath La RH12 35 G4
North Holmes Cl RH12 35 G4
North Mead RH10 11 H3
North Par RH12 34 C5
North Rd, Crawley RH10 12 A4
North Rd,
Haywards Heath RH16 25 E6
North St RH12 37 E1
North Terminal Approach Rd
RH6 8 A1
North Way RH6 8 A1
Northdown Cl RH12 35 F5
Northdown Ter*,
Dormans Park Rd RH19 20 B2
Northern Breach RH17 23 B3
Northgate Av RH10 3 E1
Northgate Pl RH10 11 H4
Northgate Rd RH10 3 C1
Northlands Av RH16 25 F6
Northlands RH12 35 E2
Northway RH15 29 G3
Northwood Pk,
Crawley RH10 12 B1
Northwood Pk,
Crawley RH10 12 B1
Norwich Rd RH10 16 B1
Norwood Hill Rd RH6 6 B2
Nursery Cl,
Hassocks BN6 31 E2
Nursery Cl,
Haywards Heath RH16 24 B6
Nursery La RH6 4 A5
Nurserylands RH11 10 D6
Nuthatch Way RH12 34 D2
Nuthurst Cl RH11 10 D4
Nye La BN6 33 G4
Nye Rd RH15 29 F3
Nymans Cl RH12 35 F2
Nymans Rd RH16 16 B2

Oak Bank RH16 24 D3
Oak Cl RH10 22 A5
Oak Croft RH19 21 F5
Oak Dell RH10 12 D4
Oak Hall Pk RH15 29 E6
Oak La RH12 38 C2
Oak Rd RH11 3 A3
Oak Tree Way RH13 35 F6
Oakapple Cl RH11 15 E5
Oakdale RH16 27 E1
Oakenfield RH15 28 D2
Oakfield RH16 25 E3
Oakfield Way RH10 20 D2
Oakfields RH10 12 D4
Oakhaven RH10 15 G1
Oakhill Rd RH13 37 E1
Oakhurst RH16 24 C3
Oakhurst Gdns RH19 20 A3
Oakhurst La RH16 24 C3
Oakhurst Mews RH13 35 G5
Oaklands RH6 5 F3
Oaklands Cl RH13 37 F3
Oaklands Rd RH16 24 B5
Oakleigh Rd RH12 35 F5
Oakley Cl RH10 21 G5
Oakmead Rd RH15 28 C6
Oakroyd Cl RH15 29 G1
Oaks Cl RH12 35 G3
Oakside Cl RH6 5 F3
Oakside La RH6 5 F3
Oakway RH10 11 G4
Oakwood Cl RH15 29 F4
Oakwood Ind Est
RH10 12 B2
Oakwood Rd,
Burgess Hill RH15 29 E4
Oakwood Rd,
Haywards Heath RH16 24 B6
Oakwood Rd,
Horley RH6 4 D3
Oates Walk RH10 15 H2
Oathall Av RH16 24 D5
Oathall Rd RH16 24 C6
Oatlands, Crawley RH11 10 D6
Oatlands, Horley RH6 5 E3
Oberon Way RH11 14 B2
Ockenden La RH17 23 B4
Ockenden Way BN6 32 B3
Ockley La BN6 32 D3
Ockley Way BN6 32 D2
Old Barn Ct RH16 26 B3
Old Brighton Rd RH11 7 H5
Old Control Tower Rd
RH6 7 F3
Old Crawley Rd RH12 35 H3
Old Denne Gdns RH12 36 D2
Old Guildford Rd RH12 38 B1
Old Holbrook RH12 35 E1
Old Hollow RH10 13 F5
Old Horsham RH12 15 E1
Old Manor Cl RH11 10 D3
Old Martyrs*,
Martyrs Av RH11 11 G2
Old Millmeads RH12 34 C4
Old Orchards RH10 13 E6
Old Park Cl RH17 23 C4
Old Rd RH19 21 E4
Old School Pl RH15 28 D5
Old Station Cl RH10 18 C6
Old Wickham La RH16 24 C3
Old Wickhurst La RH12 38 C3
Oldbury Cl RH12 35 G2
Oldfield Cl RH6 4 C6
Oldfield Rd RH6 4 C6
Oldlands Av,
Hassocks BN6 32 D2
Oldlands Av,
Haywards Heath RH17 17 B6
Oliver Rd RH12 36 B3
Olivier Rd RH10 17 E1
Onslow Ct RH10 12 B2
Orchard Cl,
Haywards Heath RH16 24 C2
Orchard Cl, Horley RH6 4 C3
Orchard Corner RH6 25 F5
Orchard Cotts RH17 23 B3
Orchard Cotts*,
Chapel Rd RH17 6 C2
Orchard La,
Ditchling BN6 33 F1
Orchard La,
Hassocks BN6 32 C2
Orchard Rd,
Burgess Hill RH15 28 B4
Orchard Rd,
Horsham RH13 37 F2
Orchard St RH11 3 B2
Orchard Way,
Burgess Hill RH15 28 C4
Orchard Way,
East Grinstead RH19 20 C4
Orchard Way,
Hassocks BN6 30 D3
Orchard Way,
Haywards Heath RH16 24 B2
Orchid Pk RH16 27 G1
Orde Cl RH10 12 D2
Oriel Cl RH10 12 D2
Orion Cl RH11 14 A2
Orion Par BN6 32 C3
Ormerod Ct RH16 24 C6
Ormesbury Walk*,
Norwich Rd RH10 16 B1
Osmund Cl RH10 13 E6
Osney Cl RH11 15 F5
Otford Cl RH10 15 F5
Ottield Ct RH16 24 D4
Otway Cl RH11 14 C2
Oulton Walk*,
Norwich Rd RH10 16 B1
Overdene Dr RH11 10 D5
Overton Shaw RH19 20 D1
Owen Cl RH15 28 C5
Owers Cl RH13 37 F1
Owlbeech Pl RH13 35 H5
Owlbeech Way RH13 35 H5
Owlcastle Cl RH12 34 D4
Owletts RH10 12 D4
Oxford Rd,
Crawley RH10 15 H3
Oxford Rd,
Horsham RH13 37 E1
Packer Cl RH19 21 E1
Packham Way RH15 28 D2
Paddock Gdns RH19 20 D6
Paddockhall Rd RH16 24 B6
Paddockhurst Rd RH11 10 C6
Padstow Walk RH11 14 B2
Padwick Rd RH13 37 G1
Paget Cl RH13 37 F3
Pagewood Cl RH10 17 E2
Pallingham Dr RH11 16 C3
Palmer Cl RH6 4 C1
Palmer Rd RH10 16 C3
Pangdene Cl RH15 28 C6
Pannell Cl RH19 20 C4
Pannett RH15 28 B2
Parham Rd RH11 10 C4
Parish Ho RH11 3 B4
Park Av BN6 32 D4
Park Cl,
Burgess Hill RH15 28 D3
Park Cl, Hassocks BN6 31 E3
Park Ct,
Burgess Hill RH15 28 D3
Park Ct,
Haywards Heath RH16 24 C4
Park Farm Cl RH12 34 D2
Park Farm Rd RH12 34 D2
Park La,
East Grinstead RH19 22 B2
Park La,
Haywards Heath RH16 25 G1
Park Pl RH12 36 D2
Park Rd,
Burgess Hill RH15 28 D3
Park Rd,
East Grinstead RH19 20 C3
Park Rd,
Haywards Heath RH16 26 C1
Park Rise RH12 34 B5
Park St RH12 36 D1
Park Ter RH13 37 E2
Park Ter West RH12 36 D2
Park View Gdns RH19 20 C1
Park Vw, Crawley RH11 11 F6
Park Vw,
Haywards Heath RH16 24 C5
Park Vw, Horley RH6 4 D4
Park Way RH12 36 D2
Parker Cl RH11 16 D1
Parkfield RH12 34 C6
Parkfield Cl RH11 10 C6
Parkfield Way RH16 26 A1
Parkhurst Gro RH6 4 C3
Parkhurst Rd RH6 4 B3
Parklands Rd RH16 32 B3
Parklawn Av RH6 4 C2
Parkside, Crawley RH10 3 D2
Parkside,
East Grinstead RH19 20 B4
Parkside, Hassocks BN6 32 C2
Parkside Mews RH12 37 E1
Parkview BN6 31 E4
Parkway, Crawley RH10 12 C3
Parkway, Horley RH6 4 D4
Parnell Cl RH11 16 D1
Parry Cl RH13 35 H5
Parsonage Bsns Pk
RH12 35 E5
Parsonage Rd RH12 34 D5
Parsonage Way RH12 35 E5
Parsons Cl RH6 4 B3
Parsons Walk RH12 36 A3
Parthings La RH13 36 A3
Pasture Hill Rd RH16 24 B4
Patching Cl RH11 10 C4
Patchings RH13 37 G1
Path Link RH10 3 E1
Patrington Cl RH11 14 D2
Patterdale Cl RH11 15 E2
Pavilion Cl BN6 32 A1
Pavilion Way RH11 20 D4
Pax Cl RH11 14 B1
Payne Cl RH10 13 E3
Payton Dr RH15 28 C5
Peacemaker Cl RH11 14 B1
Peacock Walk RH11 14 D2
Pear Tree Cl RH15 28 C4
Pearson Rd RH10 12 C5
Peary Cl RH12 34 D3
Peeks La RH6 9 E2
Pegasus Ct RH11 14 B2
Pegasus Way RH19 21 F2
Pegler Way RH11 3 B2
Pegwell Cl RH11 14 C2
Pelham Ct,
Crawley RH11 15 E3
Pelham Ct,
Horsham RH12 36 C1
Pelham Dr RH11 14 D3
Pelham Pl,
Crawley RH11 15 E3
Pelham Pl,
Haywards Heath RH16 25 E3
Pelland Rd RH16 24 B4
Pembley Grn RH10 22 D6
Pembroke Rd RH10 12 C2
Pembury Ct RH16 27 F1
Pendean RH15 29 F6
Penfold Rd RH10 16 C3
Penhurst Cl*,
Lytton Dr RH11 13 E4
Penland Cl RH16 24 B4
Penland Rd RH16 24 B3
Penn Cl RH11 11 G2
Penn Cres RH16 25 E5
Pennine Cl RH11 11 E5
Peppard Rd RH10 16 D2
Pepper Dr RH15 28 D6
Percy Rd RH12 34 B6
Perimeter Rd East RH6 8 B2
Perimeter Rd North RH6 7 G1
Perimeter Rd South RH6 7 F5
Perkstead Ct*,
Gunning Cl RH11 14 D2
Perry Av RH19 20 D2
Perryfield Ho RH11 3 B4
Perryfield Rd RH11 3 B4
Perryfields RH15 28 C2
Perrylands RH6 6 C2
Perrymount Rd RH16 24 C6
Perth Cl RH10 11 G2
Perth Way RH12 35 F5
Peterborough Rd RH13 15 H3
Peterhouse Par RH10 12 C3
Peterlee Walk*,
Basildon Way RH11 14 B3
Petlands Gdns RH16 26 D1
Petlands Rd RH16 26 D1
Petworth Ct RH11 14 C2
Petworth Dr,
Burgess Hill RH15 29 E2
Petworth Dr,
Horsham RH12 35 F2
Pevensey Cl RH10 12 C6
Peverel Rd RH11 10 B6
Phillips Cl RH10 16 C4
Phoenix La RH19 22 C2
Pickers Grn RH11 25 E2
Pierpoint Cl BN6 30 D2
Pilgrim Cl RH15 25 E5
Pine Cl RH11 11 F2
Pine Gdns RH6 4 D5
Pine Gro RH19 20 A1
Pine Shaw RH10 12 D4
Pine Tree Cl RH6 31 F4
Pine Trees BN6 32 A2
Pine Way Cl RH19 20 D6
Pineham Copse RH16 24 D6
Pinehurst,
Burgess Hill RH15 29 E6
Pinehurst,
Horsham RH12 34 C5
Pinetops RH13 35 H5
Pinetrees Cl RH10 22 B5
Pinewood Cl RH12 38 B2
Pinewood Cl RH16 26 B3
Pinewood Way RH16 26 B3
Piries Pl RH12 36 D1
Pitt La BN6 31 E4
Plantain Cres RH11 14 D3
Playden Ct RH11 14 C3
Plough Cl RH11 10 C4
Plough La RH12 34 D5
Plover Cl RH11 11 F3
Plovers Rd RH13 35 F6
Poles La RH11 7 F5
Polestub La RH11 23 B2
Policemans La BN6 30 D3
Pollards RH11 10 D6
Pollards Dr RH13 37 F1
Pond Wood Rd RH10 12 B3
Pondcroft Rd RH16 25 F3
Pondside RH16 26 A1
Pondtail Cl RH12 34 C3
Pondtail Copse RH12 34 D3
Pondtail Dr RH12 34 D2
Pondtail Rd RH12 34 C3
Poplar Cl RH11 11 F2
Portland Rd,
Burgess Hill RH15 28 C4
Portland Rd,
East Grinstead RH19 20 D5
Portsmouth La RH16 24 D2
Portsmouth Wood
RH16 24 D2
Portsmouth Wood Cl
RH16 24 D2
Potters Cft RH13 37 F1
Potters La RH15 28 D6
Potters Pl RH12 36 C1
Pound Gate BN6 32 A3
Pound Hill Pl RH10 12 D5
Povey Cross Rd RH6 4 B6
Poveys Cl RH6 28 B3
Powell RH6 4 B3
Poynes Rd RH6 4 B2
Poynings Rd RH11 10 B6
Prescott Gdns RH15 28 D3
Prestwick Cl RH11 10 A6
Prestwood Cl RH11 11 E2
Prestwood La RH11 6 A6
Priestcroft Cl RH11 10 D6
Priestley Way RH10 8 A6
Primrose Av RH6 5 E6
Primrose Cl,
Burgess Hill RH15 28 B2
Primrose Cl,
Crawley RH11 15 E3
Primrose Copse RH12 34 D3
Princess Rd RH11 3 A2
Priors Walk RH10 3 E2
Priory Cl RH6 4 C5
Priory Rd,
Burgess Hill RH15 28 D6
Priory Rd,
Hassocks BN6 32 B1
Priory Way RH16 24 D6
Proctor Dr RH10 16 C1
Prospect Ct RH11 3 A2
Pudding La RH6 6 B2
Puffin Rd RH11 10 A4
Punch Copse Rd RH10 12 A4
Punnetts Ct RH11 14 C3
Purcell Rd RH11 14 C3
Purley Cl RH10 16 D2
Purton Rd RH12 34 B5
Pyecombe Ct RH11 14 C3
Quail Cl RH12 34 D2
Quakers La RH16 25 E6
Quantock Cl RH11 11 E5
Quarry Cl,
Burgess Hill RH15 29 G4
Quarry Cl,
Horsham RH12 35 F2
Quarry Hill RH16 24 A6
Quarry Rise RH19 21 E2
Quarterbrass Farm Rd
RH12 34 D3
Queen Elizabeth Av
RH15 37 E1
Queen St RH13 37 E1
Queens Cres RH11 29 E1
Queens Cl RH16 24 D6
Queens Dr BN6 32 C3
Queens Gate RH6 8 B1
Queens Rd,
East Grinstead RH19 20 D4
Queens Rd,
Haywards Heath RH16 24 C4
Queens Rd, Horley RH6 4 D4
Queens Sq RH10 20 D4
Queens Walk RH19 20 D4
Queens Way RH19 20 D4
Queensway,
Crawley RH10 3 D4
Queensway,
Horsham RH13 36 D4
Questen Mews RH10 13 E2
Racecourse Way RH6 8 A4
Rackham Cl RH11 15 F4
Radford Rd RH10 8 B5
Railey Rd RH10 3 E3
Railway App RH19 20 C4
Rakers Ridge RH12 34 D3
Raleigh Ct RH10 12 B3
Raleigh Walk RH10 15 H4
Ramblers Way RH11 15 E3
Ramsey Cl, Horley RH6 4 D4
Ramsey Cl,
Horsham RH12 34 D4
Ramsey Ct RH11 15 E4
Randall Scofield Ct*,
Crossways RH10 12 C3
Randiddles Cl BN6 31 F3
Ranmore Cl RH11 14 D3
Ransome Cl RH11 14 E3
Rastrick Cl RH15 28 C4

Rathlin Rd RH11 15 E3
Raven Cl RH12 35 E3
Raven La RH11 11 F3
Ravendene Ct RH11 3 B3
Ravenscroft Ct RH12 34 C6
Ravenswood BN6 32 B2
Ravenswood Rd RH15 29 F4
Raworth Cl RH10 16 C1
Raymer Walk RH6 5 F3
Reapers Cl RH12 34 D4
Rectory La, Crawley RH11 10 C3
Rectory La, Horley RH6 6 A3
Red Admiral St RH12 35 E4
Red Deer Cl RH13 35 G6
Red River Ct RH12 34 B4
Redditch Cl RH11 14 B3
Redford Av RH12 34 B5
Redgarth Ct RH19 20 A1
Redgrave Dr RH10 12 D6
Redkiln Cl RH13 35 E6
Redkiln Way RH13 35 E5
Redshank Ct*, Fairway RH11 14 A1
Redwing Cl RH13 35 F6
Redwood Cl RH10 11 G3
Redwood Dr RH16 26 C2
Reed Pond Walk RH16 27 E1
Reedings RH11 14 A1
Reeds La BN6 30 A1
Regal Dr RH19 21 E5
Regent Bsns Pk RH15 28 B5
Regents Cl RH11 15 F3
Reigate Cl RH10 13 E3
Reigate Rd RH6 4 A4
Renfields RH16 26 A2
Reynard Cl RH12 35 G4
Reynolds Pl RH11 11 E4
Reynolds Rd RH11 11 E5
Rhodes Way RH10 15 H2
Rices Hill RH19 20 D4
Richardson Ct RH11 15 E4
Richborough Ct RH11 3 A2
Richmond Ct RH10 3 D4
Richmond Rd RH12 34 C6
Richmond Sq RH19 20 C2
Richmond Way RH19 21 E5
Rickfield RH11 10 D6
Rickwood RH6 5 E3
Ridge Way RH17 27 F2
Ridgehurst Dr RH12 36 A2
Ridgeside RH10 3 F2
Ridgeway, East Grinstead RH19 20 D5
Ridgeway, Horsham RH12 34 B5
Rillside RH10 16 A2
Rimmer Cl RH11 15 E5
Ring Rd North RH6 8 C2
Ring Rd South RH6 8 C2
Ringley Av RH6 4 D4
Ringley Oak RH12 35 E5
Ringley Rd RH12 35 E5
Ringwood Cl RH10 15 H1
Ritchie Cl RH10 16 C3
River Mead, Crawley RH11 10 D2
River Mead, Horsham RH12 36 C2
Riverside, Horley RH6 4 D6
Riverside, Horsham RH12 36 B1
Robert Way RH12 35 E2
Robin Cl, Crawley RH11 11 F3
Robin Cl, East Grinstead RH19 20 D3
Robin Hood La RH12 34 A4
Robin Rd RH15 28 A4
Robinson Rd RH11 3 B3
Robinswood Ct RH12 35 E5
Rocks La RH17 17 B6
Rocky La RH16 26 A4
Roebuck Cl RH13 35 G5
Roffey Cl RH6 4 C4
Roffeys Cl RH10 22 A5
Roffye Ct RH12 35 F5
Rolfe Dr RH15 29 G4
Romaine Cl RH15 29 G2
Rona Cl RH11 15 E2
Rook Way RH12 35 E3
Rookery Way RH16 26 C3
Rookwood Pk RH12 34 A6
Ropeland Way RH12 35 E2
Rosamund Rd RH10 16 B2
Rose Way RH11 15 E1
Rosebarn Cl RH15 29 G6
Rosedale Cl RH11 14 D1
Rosemary Cl RH16 24 A5
Rosemary Ct RH6 4 B3
Rosemary La, Charlwood RH6 6 B2
Rosemary La, Horley RH6 5 E5
Roslan Ct RH6 5 E5
Ross Cl RH10 16 A2
Rossmore Cl RH10 13 E1
Rother Cres RH11 10 C6
Rothervale RH6 4 C1
Rothley Chase RH16 26 D1
Rough Fld RH19 20 C1
Rough Way RH12 35 F4
Roundway Ct*, London Rd RH11 11 G3
Roundwood La RH16 24 D2
Rowan Cl, Crawley RH10 3 F2
Rowan Cl, Haywards Heath RH16 27 F1
Rowan Cl, Horsham RH12 35 H4
Rowan Walk RH10 18 D6
Rowan Way RH12 35 H4
Rowfant Cl RH10 13 E5
Rowlands Rd RH12 35 F3
Rowplatt La RH19 19 F2
Royal George Rd RH15 28 B3
Royce Rd RH10 12 A1
Royston Cl RH10 12 B2
Rudgwick Keep*, Langshott La RH6 5 E3
Rudgwick Rd RH11 10 C5
Rufwood RH10 18 B5
Rumbolds La RH16 26 B3
Runcorn Cl RH11 14 B3
Runshooke Ct RH11 14 D2
Rushams Rd RH12 34 B6
Rushetts Pl RH11 11 F2
Rushetts Rd RH11 11 E3
Rushhams Rd RH12 36 C1
Rushwood Cl RH16 27 F1
Ruskin Cl RH10 12 C3
Rusper Rd, Crawley RH11 10 A4
Rusper Rd, Horsham RH12 35 E5
Ruspers RH15 29 G5
Ruspers Keep RH11 10 C4
Russ Hill Rd RH6 6 A3
Russell Way RH10 12 A6
Russells Cres RH6 4 D5
Russet Cl RH6 5 F3
Rustlings Cl RH16 25 F5
Ruston Cl RH10 16 C2
Rutherford Way RH10 8 B6
Rutherwick Cl RH6 4 C4
Ruthven Cl RH17 23 B2
Rydal Cl RH11 14 A1
Ryders Way RH12 35 E2
Rye Ash RH10 12 B4
Ryecroft RH16 26 C1
Ryecroft Dr RH12 34 A6
Ryelands, Crawley RH11 10 D6
Ryelands, Horley RH6 5 E3

Sackville Cl RH19 20 B1
Sackville Ct RH19 21 E4
Sackville Gdns RH19 20 B2
Sackville La RH19 20 A2
Saddler Row RH10 15 G2
Saddlers Cl RH15 29 G6
Saffron Cl RH11 14 D3
St Agnes Rd RH19 20 C3
St Andrews Rd, Burgess Hill RH15 29 F3
St Andrews Rd, Crawley RH11 10 A6
St Annes Gdns BN6 32 D3
St Annes Rd RH10 12 D2
St Aubin Cl RH11 14 C3
St Barnabas Ct*, Crawley La RH10 12 C4
St Brelades Rd RH11 14 C3
St Catherines Rd RH10 12 D2
St Christophers Cl RH12 34 C5
St Christophers Rd BN6 31 E3
St Clement Rd RH11 14 C3
St Edmund Cl RH11 11 G2
St Edmunds Rd RH16 26 D1
St Edwards Cl RH19 20 B4
St Francis Cl RH16 26 D2
St Francis Gdns RH10 22 B5
St Francis Walk RH11 14 B1
St Georges Cl RH6 5 E4
St Georges Ct, Crawley RH10 11 G4
St Georges Ct, East Grinstead RH19 20 B2
St Georges Gdns RH13 35 E5
St Georges La BN6 31 F4
St Georges Pl BN6 31 F4
St Helena La RH15 29 H6
St Helier Cl RH11 14 D3
St Hildas Cl, Crawley RH10 12 D2
St Hildas Cl, Horley RH6 4 D3
St Hughs Cl RH10 12 D2
St James Rd RH19 20 C3
St James Walk RH11 15 F4
St Joan Cl RH11 11 G2
St Johns Av RH15 28 D3
St Johns Cl, East Grinstead RH19 20 D3
St Johns Cl, Horsham RH13 37 E2
St Johns Cres RH12 38 C2
St Johns Ct RH15 28 D4
St Johns Rd, Crawley RH11 3 A2
St Johns Rd, East Grinstead RH19 20 D3
St Johns Rd, Haywards Heath RH16 26 D2
St Josephs Way RH16 24 C6
St Lawrence Way BN6 31 E2
St Leonards Dr RH10 16 B2
St Leonards Pk RH19 20 C4
St Leonards Rd RH13 37 F3
St Margarets Rd RH19 21 E2
St Marks La RH12 35 E3
St Marys Dr RH10 12 C3
St Marys Gdns RH12 36 D2
St Marys Rd RH15 28 C3
St Marys Rd West RH15 28 C3
St Michaels Rd RH19 20 D3
St Nicholas Ct*, Crawley La RH10 12 C4
St Pauls Cl RH16 24 D5
St Peters Rd, Burgess Hill RH15 29 E3
St Peters Rd, Crawley RH11 3 A2
St Sampson Rd RH11 14 C3
St Stephen Cl RH11 11 G2
St Swithuns Cl RH19 21 E4
St Vincent Cl RH10 12 D6
St Wilfrids Rd RH15 29 E3
St Wilfrids Way RH16 24 C6
Salehurst Rd RH10 13 E5
Salisbury Rd, Crawley RH10 15 H4
Salisbury Rd, Horsham RH13 36 B4
Saltdean Cl RH11 15 F2
Salterns Rd RH10 16 C2
Salvington Rd RH11 14 C3
Samaritan Cl RH11 14 B1
Samphire Cl RH11 14 D3
San Feliu Ct RH19 21 F3
Sandeman Way RH13 37 F3
Sandhawes Hill RH19 21 F1
Sandhill La RH10 18 C6
Sandpiper Cl RH11 14 A1
Sandridge La RH16 24 D1
Sandringham Cl RH19 21 E5
Sandringham Rd RH11 15 E3
Sandrocks Way RH16 26 C2
Sandy La, Crawley RH10 18 B5
Sandy La, East Grinstead RH19 20 D3
Sandy Vale RH16 26 C2
Sandy Way RH16 26 C2
Sangers Dr RH6 4 C4
Sarel Way RH6 5 E2
Sargent Cl RH10 16 A3
Sark Cl RH11 14 D3
Saturn Cl RH11 14 B2
Saunders Cl RH10 12 C5
Savernake Walk RH10 16 A2
Savill Rd RH16 25 E2
Sawyers Cl RH15 29 G5
Saxby Rd RH15 28 B2
Saxley RH6 5 F3
Saxon Cres RH12 34 B5
Saxon Rd RH10 13 E6
Sayers Cl RH13 37 F1
Scallows Cl RH10 12 A4
Scallows Rd RH10 12 A4
Scamps Hill RH16 25 G4
Scholars Ct RH10 18 B6
School Cl, Burgess Hill RH15 28 D4
School Cl, Horsham RH12 35 G3
School La RH19 22 B2
Scory Cl RH11 14 D2
Scott Rd RH10 15 H2
Seaford Rd RH11 14 D4
Searles Vw RH12 35 E4
Seddon Ct*, Chippendale Rd RH11 15 E4
Sedgefield Cl RH10 13 E4
Sedgewick Cl RH10 12 D5
Selbourne Cl RH10 12 D2
Selby Ct RH16 26 C1
Selham Cl RH11 10 D5
Selsey Rd RH11 14 D4
Selwyn Cl RH10 12 D2
Semley Rd BN6 32 B2
Sequoia Pk RH11 15 F1
Sergison Cl RH16 24 B5
Sergison Rd RH16 24 B5
Serrin Way RH12 35 E4
Sevenfields RH15 28 A3
Severn Rd RH10 12 C6
Sewill Cl RH6 6 C2
Seymour Rd RH11 14 D3
Shackleton Rd RH10 15 H2
Shaftesbury Rd RH10 16 D1
Shandys Cl RH12 36 B2
Sharon Cl RH10 16 B2
Sharpthorne Cl RH11 10 C5
Sharrow Cl RH16 24 C6
Shaws Rd RH10 11 H4
Shearwater Ct*, Fairway RH11 14 A1
Sheddingdean Ct RH15 28 D2
Sheddingdean Ind Est RH15 28 D1
Sheffield Cl RH10 16 B1
Sheldon Cl RH10 16 D1
Shelley Cl RH10 12 C4
Shelley Ct RH16 24 C5
Shelley Dr RH12 38 B2
Shelley Rd, East Grinstead RH19 20 B4
Shelley Rd, Horsham RH12 34 B6
Shelley Wood RH15 28 A3
Shelleys Ct RH13 35 G6
Shenstone RH16 25 F2
Shepherd Cl RH10 15 G2
Shepherds Mead RH15 28 C2
Shepherds Walk BN6 32 B1
Shepherds Way RH12 35 G4
Sheppey Cl RH11 15 E3
Sheppeys RH16 26 B2
Sheridan Pl RH19 20 B4
Sherwood Dr RH16 24 A5
Sherwood Walk RH10 16 A2
Shetland Cl RH10 13 E4
Ship St RH19 20 D5
Shipley Bridge La RH10 9 F5
Shipley Rd RH11 10 C5
Shire Par RH10 13 E4
Shirley Cl RH11 14 B3
Shirleys BN6 33 G4
Shoreham Rd RH10 16 D2
Short Cl RH11 11 G3
Shorts Cl RH16 26 C1
Shortsfield Cl RH12 34 C4
Shottermill RH12 35 G2
Shotters RH15 28 C5
Silchester Dr RH11 15 E2
Silkin Walk RH11 15 E4
Silver Birches RH16 25 E6
Silverdale BN6 32 D3
Silverdale Rd RH15 29 E5
Silverlea Gdns RH6 5 E5
Sinclair Cl RH10 16 C1
Singleton Rd RH12 38 B2
Singleton Way RH15 29 F6
Siskin Cl RH12 35 E4
Sissinghurst Cl RH10 13 E5
Skelmersdale Walk RH11 14 B3
Skipton Way RH6 5 E2
Skylark Vw RH12 34 D2
Slaugham Ct RH11 14 C2
Sleets Rd RH12 38 C2
Slimbridge Rd RH15 28 C3
Slinfold Walk RH11 10 D5
Sloughbrook Cl RH12 35 F3
Slugwash La RH17 27 F6
Smallfield Rd RH6 5 E4
Smallmead RH6 5 E4
Smalls La RH11 3 B2
Smalls Mead RH11 3 A2
Smalls Mead St RH11 11 F5
Smith Cl RH10 15 G2
Smithbarn RH13 37 G1
Smithbarn Cl RH6 5 E2
Smolletts RH19 20 B4
Snell Hatch RH11 11 E5
Snow Hill RH10 18 A1
Snow Hill La RH10 18 B1
Snowdrop Cl RH11 14 D3
Snowdrop La RH16 25 G6
Snowflakes La RH16 25 H4
Soane Cl RH11 14 B1
Somergate RH12 36 A1
Somerville Rd RH10 12 D3
Sorrel Cl RH11 14 D3
Sorrell Rd RH12 34 D4
South Av BN6 31 E4
South Bank BN6 32 A3
South Cl, Burgess Hill RH15 28 B3
South Cl, Crawley RH10 11 H4
South Dr RH15 28 B3
South Gro RH13 37 E2
South Holmes Rd RH13 35 G5
South Lodge Cl RH15 28 C2
South Parade RH6 4 C3
South Rd RH16 24 C6
South St, Hassocks BN6 33 F3
South St, Haywards Heath RH17 23 B4
South St, Horsham RH12 36 D2
Southbrook RH11 15 F5
Southdown Cl, Haywards Heath RH16 26 C2
Southdown Cl, Horsham RH12 35 G4
Southgate Av RH10 3 D3
Southgate Dr RH10 15 G1
Southgate Rd RH10 15 G1
Southlands, East Grinstead RH19 20 C6
Southlands, Horley RH6 4 C4
Southlands Av RH6 4 C3
Southview BN6 33 G1
Southview Cl RH10 18 A2
Southwark Cl*, Sandringham Rd RH11 15 E3
Southwater Cl RH11 10 D5
Southway, Burgess Hill RH15 28 B4
Southway, Horley RH6 8 C2
Southwick Cl RH19 20 C3
Sovereign Bsns Pk RH15 28 C5
Spanish Ct RH15 29 E3
Sparrow Way RH15 28 A4
Spatham La BN6 33 H4
Speedwell Way RH12 35 E4
Spencers Pl RH12 34 B5
Spencers Rd, Crawley RH11 3 A3
Spencers Rd, Horsham RH12 34 B6
Spicers Cl RH15 28 D2
Spiers Way RH6 5 E6
Spindle Way RH10 3 E3
Spinney Cl, Crawley RH10 18 D5
Spinney Cl, Hassocks BN6 31 F4
Spinney Cl, Horsham RH12 35 H3
Spooners Rd RH12 35 F5
Spring Copse RH10 22 C5
Spring Gdns, Crawley RH10 22 C5
Spring Gdns, Horsham RH12 34 C6
Spring La, Hassocks BN6 32 B6
Spring La, Haywards Heath RH16 25 F2
Spring Plat RH10 12 C5
Spring Way RH19 21 E1
Springfield RH19 20 C1
Springfield Cres RH12 36 C1
Springfield Ct, Crawley RH11 3 B3
Springfield Ct, Horsham RH12 36 D1
Springfield Park Rd RH12 36 C1
Springfield Pk RH12 34 C6
Springfield Rd, Crawley RH11 3 A3
Springfield Rd, Horsham RH12 36 C1
Spurgeon Cl RH11 3 A1
Squires Cl RH10 18 B5
Squirrel Cl RH11 11 E2
Stable Cl RH10 16 D2
Stace Way RH10 13 E3
Stackfield Rd RH11 14 B1
Stafford Rd RH11 10 D2
Stafford Way BN6 32 C3
Staffords Pl RH6 5 E5
Stagelands RH11 11 E3
Stan Hill RH6 6 A1
Stanbridge Cl RH11 10 B6
Standen Cl RH19 19 H2
Standen Pl RH12 35 F2
Stanford Av BN6 32 A2
Stanford Cl BN6 32 A2
Stanford Cl RH10 16 D1
Stanford Ter BN6 32 B2
Stanford Way RH12 38 B2
Stanier Cl RH10 12 C6
Stanley Centre RH10 12 A2
Stanley Cl RH10 15 H2
Stanley Walk RH13 37 E2
Stans Way RH12 36 D2
Staplecross Ct RH11 14 C3

Staplefield Rd RH17 23 A1
Star Cl RH13 35 F5
Starleys BN6 30 B3
Starling Cl RH15 28 A4
Station App,
 Hassocks BN6 32 B2
Station App, Horley RH6 5 E4
Station Approach Rd
 RH6 8 B1
Station Cl RH13 37 E1
Station Cotts BN6 32 B2
Station Hill RH10 12 C5
Station Rd,
 Burgess Hill RH15 28 D5
Station Rd,
 Crawley RH10 3 C3
Station Rd,
 Crawley Down RH10 18 C5
Station Rd,
 East Grinstead RH19 20 C4
Station Rd, Horley RH6 5 E4
Station Rd,
 Horsham RH13 37 E1
Station Rd,
 Warnham RH12 34 A1
Station Way RH10 3 C3
Steers La RH10 8 C5
Stephenson Dr RH19 20 D6
Stephenson Pl RH10 12 B6
Stephenson Way RH10 12 B6
Stevenage Rd RH11 14 B3
Steyning Cl RH10 11 H3
Stirling Cl,
 Burgess Hill RH15 29 F2
Stirling Cl,
 Crawley RH10 16 C1
Stirling Court Rd RH15 29 F2
Stirling Way,
 East Grinstead RH19 21 F1
Stirling Way,
 Horsham RH13 37 F1
Stirrup Way RH10 13 E4
Stockcroft Rd RH17 17 C5
Stockfield RH6 5 E3
Stocklands Cl RH17 23 C2
Stocks Cl RH6 5 E5
Stockwell Ct RH16 26 C1
Stokes Cl RH10 16 D2
Stonebridge Ct RH12 36 C2
Stonecourt Cl RH6 5 F4
Stonecrop Cl RH11 14 D2
Stonefield Cl RH11 3 C4
Stonefield Way RH15 28 D2
Stoneleigh Cl RH19 21 E3
Stonepound Rd BN6 32 A2
Stoners RH6 7 G1
Stoneybrook RH12 36 A2
Stoneycroft Walk*,
 Fairway RH11 14 A1
Stopham Rd RH10 16 C2
Storrington Ct RH11 10 D4
Strand RH10 16 D1
Strathfield Cl RH16 26 D1
Strathmore Rd RH11 10 D2
Stream Pk RH19 19 H2
Street Hill RH10 13 E6
Strickland Cl RH11 10 B6
Stroudley Cl RH10 12 C6
Strudgate Cl RH10 16 B1
Stuart Cl RH10 12 D6
Stuart Way RH19 21 E5
Stubfield RH12 34 A6
Stumblemead RH17 17 C6
Stumblets RH10 12 D4
Suffolk Cl RH6 4 D5
Sugworth Cl RH16 24 B3
Sullington Hill RH15 15 F1
Sullington Mead RH12 38 C2
Sullivan Dr RH11 14 B3
Summerhill Cl RH16 24 D4
Summerhill Dr RH16 25 E3
Summerhill Grange
 RH16 24 D3
Summerhill La RH16 24 D3
Summersvere Cl RH10 12 B2
Sundew Cl RH11 14 D3
Sunningdale Ct RH11 3 B4
Sunny Av RH16 18 B6
Sunnyhill Cl RH16 18 C5
Sunnymead,
 Crawley RH11 3 B2
Sunnymead,
 Crawley Down RH10 18 C6
Sunnywood Dr RH16 26 B2
Sunset La RH15 29 E6
Sunte Av RH16 24 D3
Sunte Cl RH16 24 C3
Surrey Ct*,
 New St RH13 37 E2
Sussex Border Path RH6 6 A4
Sussex Cl RH16 26 C1
Sussex Gdns RH17 27 F2

Sussex Lodge RH12 34 C5
Sussex Manor Bsns Pk
 RH10 12 A1
Sussex Rd RH16 26 D1
Sussex Sq RH16 26 C1
Sussex Way RH15 28 B3
Swainsthorpe Cl RH16 26 D1
Swaledale Cl RH11 15 E2
Swallow Rd RH11 11 F3
Swallow Rest RH15 28 A3
Swallowtail Rd RH10 35 E3
Swan La RH16 6 C2
Swan Sq RH12 36 D1
Swan Walk RH12 36 D1
Swann Cl RH15 29 G3
Swann Way RH12 38 C2
Sweetlands BN6 32 D1
Swift Cl RH15 28 A3
Swift La RH11 11 F3
Swindon Rd RH12 34 B5
Sycamore Av RH12 35 H4
Sycamore Cl RH11 11 F7
Sycamore Dr RH11 21 F4
Sydney Rd RH16 24 C5
Sylvan Cl RH16 27 F1
Sylvan Rd RH10 16 A1
Syresham Gdns RH16 26 D1

Tallis Cl RH11 14 C2
Talman Cl RH11 14 B1
Tamar Cl RH10 12 C6
Tanbridge Pk RH12 36 C2
Tanbridge Pl RH12 36 C2
Tanfield Ct RH12 36 C1
Tangle Oak RH19 19 F1
Tangmere Rd RH11 10 C5
Tanyard Av RH19 21 E5
Tanyard Cl,
 Crawley RH10 16 C2
Tanyard Cl,
 Horsham RH13 37 E2
Tanyard Way RH6 5 E2
Tarham Cl RH6 4 B2
Tate Cres RH15 28 C2
Tatham Ct*,
 Chippendale Rd RH11 15 E4
Taunton Cl RH10 13 E5
Taylor Walk RH11 3 A1
Teal Cl RH12 34 C4
Teasel Cl RH11 15 E3
Teesdale RH11 15 F2
Telford Pl RH10 3 E3
Telham Ct RH11 14 C2
Temple Cl RH10 12 D6
Temple Gro RH15 28 B3
Tennyson Cl,
 Crawley RH10 12 C3
Tennyson Cl,
 Horsham RH12 35 E3
Tennyson Ct RH16 24 C5
Tennyson Rise RH19 20 B4
Tern Rd RH11 10 A6
Terry Rd RH11 15 E5
Thatcher Cl RH10 15 G2
Thatchers Cl,
 Burgess Hill RH15 29 G6
Thatchers Cl,
 Horley RH6 5 E2
Thatchers Cl,
 Horsham RH12 34 D5
The Acorns,
 Burgess Hill RH15 28 A2
The Acorns,
 Crawley RH11 15 E5
The Avenue,
 Crawley RH11 15 G4
The Avenue, Horley RH6 4 C5
The Belfry RH19 20 C4
The Birches RH11 12 B4
The Blackthorns RH15 29 F2
The Blytons RH19 20 A4
The Boulevard RH10 3 B3
The Bourne BN6 32 B1
The Bower,
 Crawley RH10 12 C6
The Bower,
 Haywards Heath RH16 24 B6
The Brambles RH17 23 C3
The Broadway,
 Crawley RH10 3 C2
The Broadway,
 Haywards Heath RH16 24 C6
The Brontes RH19 20 C4
The Brook RH10 11 G4
The Brooks RH15 28 C2
The Brow RH15 28 D4
The Brownings*,
 Garden Wood Rd RH19 20 E4
The Cackstones RH10 13 E4
The Canter RH10 13 E4
The Castle RH12 35 E2
The Causeway RH12 36 D2

The Cedars RH16 24 B3
The Chase RH10 16 A1
The Chestnuts RH16 25 E3
The Close,
 Burgess Hill RH15 29 G3
The Close,
 East Grinstead RH19 20 B5
The Close,
 Hassocks BN6 32 C2
The Close, Horley RH6 5 F6
The Coppice RH10 18 D5
The Copse RH16 25 F6
The Coronet RH6 5 F6
The Courtyard,
 Crawley RH10 3 C3
The Courtyard,
 East Grinstead RH19 21 F4
The Covey RH10 13 E3
The Crescent,
 Hassocks BN6 32 D3
The Crescent,
 Horley RH6 4 D6
The Crescent,
 Horsham RH12 36 B2
The Croft, Crawley RH11 10 D6
The Croft,
 Hassocks BN6 32 B1
The Dakins RH19 20 D5
The Dell,
 Haywards Heath RH16 24 B5
The Dell, Horley RH6 5 E3
The Dingle RH15 11 E5
The Driftway RH11 3 B1
The Drive,
 Burgess Hill RH15 29 E3
The Drive,
 Crawley RH10 22 C5
The Drive,
 Haywards Heath RH16 24 D2
The Drive, Horley RH6 5 E5
The Drove BN6 33 F3
The Droveway RH16 24 A5
The Dymocks BN6 33 F3
The Felbridge Centre
 RH19 19 H2
The Feld RH19 19 H2
The Fieldings RH6 5 E3
The Forge RH6 6 B2
The Gables,
 Crawley RH10 22 B6
The Gables,
 Horsham RH12 34 C5
The Garrones RH10 13 E4
The Gattons RH15 28 B3
The Gilligans RH15 28 C2
The Glade,
 Crawley RH10 16 A1
The Glade,
 Horsham RH13 35 G6
The Glades RH19 21 G4
The Glebe,
 Crawley RH10 22 B5
The Glebe,
 East Grinstead RH19 19 H1
The Glebe,
 Hassocks BN6 31 E3
The Glebe,
 Haywards Heath RH16 25 E3
The Glebe, Horley RH6 4 C4
The Grange RH6 4 D1
The Green,
 Copthorne RH10 22 B5
The Green,
 Crawley RH11 11 F5
The Grooms RH10 13 E4
The Grove,
 Crawley RH11 11 F5
The Grove,
 Haywards Heath RH16 27 F1
The Grove, Horley RH6 5 E5
The Ham RH15 31 H5
The Hawthorns RH15 29 E2
The Highlands RH11 23 C1
The Hollands RH15 29 F3
The Hollow,
 Crawley RH10 10 C6
The Hollow,
 Haywards Heath RH16 25 F6
The Holt RH15 29 G5
The Hornbeams RH15 28 A2
The Jays RH15 28 C3
The Jordans RH19 20 D5
The Kiln RH15 29 G3
The Knowle RH17 23 B2
The Larches,
 East Grinstead RH19 21 F1
The Larches,
 Horsham RH12 35 H3
The Laurels RH16 24 A6
The Leas RH15 28 C3
The Limes RH19 19 H1
The Lindens RH15 22 B5

The Link RH11 3 B1
The Maltings RH15 28 A3
The Mardens RH11 11 E4
The Marlings RH16 26 A2
The Martins RH10 19 E5
The Martlets,
 Burgess Hill RH15 29 E4
The Martlets,
 Crawley RH10 3 D2
The Meadow RH10 22 A5
The Meadows BN6 32 B1
The Meads RH19 20 D6
The Meadway RH6 5 F2
The Mews RH12 38 B1
The Millbank RH11 10 C6
The Minnels BN6 32 C3
The Moorings RH19 19 H2
The Nursery RH15 29 F3
The Oaks,
 Burgess Hill RH15 28 A2
The Oaks,
 East Grinstead RH19 21 F4
The Oaks,
 Haywards Heath RH16 25 F6
The Orchard BN6 32 B3
The Orchard RH13 35 H5
The Orchard,
 Broadbridge Heath
 RH12 38 B2
The Orchards,
 Crawley RH11 14 A1
The Orchards,
 Haywards Heath RH16 24 C6
The Orchards,
 Horsham RH12 35 F4
The Paddock,
 Crawley RH10 13 E4
The Paddock,
 Horsham RH12 38 C2
The Paddocks RH16 26 A1
The Parade RH10 11 H4
The Pasture RH10 12 C6
The Pavement RH10 3 D2
The Pines,
 Haywards Heath RH16 25 F6
The Pines,
 Horsham RH12 36 B1
The Plat RH12 36 B1
The Platt RH16 25 F5
The Poplars,
 Hassocks BN6 32 C3
The Poplars,
 Horsham RH13 37 F1
The Pound RH15 28 D2
The Quadrant RH10 32 D2
The Ridgeway,
 Burgess Hill RH15 29 E2
The Ridgeway,
 Horley RH6 4 D6
The Ridings,
 Burgess Hill RH15 29 F5
The Ridings,
 Crawley RH10 13 E4
The Rise, Crawley RH10 12 D5
The Rise,
 East Grinstead RH19 20 D5
The Rise,
 Haywards Heath RH16 25 F6
The Rocks RH19 22 B2
The Rowans RH16 28 A2
The Rushes RH16 27 G1
The Saffrons RH15 28 C2
The Satellite Bsns Village
 RH10 11 H1
The Sayers RH19 20 B4
The Spinney,
 Burgess Hill RH15 29 E2
The Spinney,
 Crawley RH11 15 E1
The Spinney,
 Hassocks BN6 32 B1
The Spinney,
 Haywards Heath RH16 24 B3
The Spinney,
 Horley RH6 4 D2
The Square RH10 3 C2
The Stennings RH10 20 B2
The Street,
 Albourne BN6 30 B3
The Street,
 Ditchling BN6 33 H6
The Street, Horley RH6 6 B2
The Twitten,
 Burgess Hill RH15 29 E2
The Twitten,
 Crawley RH11 11 E5
The Twitten,
 Ditchling BN6 33 F3
The Twitten,
 Hassocks BN6 30 B3
The Vineries RH15 29 G3
The Warren RH15 29 F5

The Weald RH19 21 E1
The Welkin RH16 25 F2
The Wickets RH15 28 C2
The Wilderness RH16 25 F2
The Willows,
 Burgess Hill RH15 29 F1
The Willows,
 Horsham RH12 34 C4
Thelton Av RH12 38 B2
Theobalds Rd,
 Burgess Hill RH15 28 B6
Theobalds Rd,
 Burgess Hill RH15 29 F1
Thetford Walk RH11 14 B3
Theydon Ct RH10 16 A1
Thirlmere Rd RH11 14 A1
Thompson Ct*,
 Chadwick Ct RH15 15 E4
Thorndyke Cl RH10 16 D1
Thornhill RH11 15 E1
Thornton Cl RH6 4 B3
Thornton Pl RH6 4 B4
Three Acres RH12 36 B2
Three Bridges Rd RH10 3 E2
Ticehurst Cl RH10 13 F5
Tilers Cl RH15 29 G3
Tilgate Dr,
 Crawley RH10 12 B6
Tilgate Dr,
 Crawley RH10 15 G4
Tilgate Forest Bsns Centre
 RH11 15 F4
Tilgate Par RH10 15 H2
Tilgate Pl RH10 15 H2
Tilgate Way RH10 15 H2
Tillotson Cl RH10 12 D6
Tiltwood Dr RH10 18 D5
Timber Cl RH12 34 C6
Timberham Farm Rd
 RH6 7 G1
Timberham Link RH6 7 H1
Timberham Way RH6 7 G1
Timberlands RH11 15 E6
Tindal Cl RH11 29 G4
Tinsley Cl RH10 12 B2
Tinsley Grn RH10 8 C4
Tinsley La RH10 12 B2
Tinsley La North RH10 8 B6
Tinsley La South RH10 12 B3
Tintern Rd RH11 14 D2
Tiree Path RH11 15 E3
Titchfield Cl RH10 29 G4
Tithe Orch RH19 19 F1
Titmus Dr RH10 15 H2
Tollgate Rd RH16 25 F7
Tollgate Hill RH11 15 E6
Tollgate La RH17 23 B6
Tott Hill BN6 31 F5
Tower Cl,
 East Grinstead RH19 20 C5
Tower Cl, Horley RH6 4 C6
Tower Cl,
 Horsham RH13 36 B5
Tower Ct*,
 Tower Cl RH19 20 D5
Tower Hill RH13 36 B6
Tower House Cl RH17 23 B6
Town Barn Rd RH11 3 A2
Town Ct RH11 3 B4
Town Mead RH11 3 B4
Trafalgar Rd RH12 34 B5
Treadcroft Dr RH12 35 E4
Treeview RH15 15 F3
Trefoil Cl RH12 34 B6
Trefoil Cres RH11 14 D4
Trenear Cl RH13 37 F1
Trent Cl RH11 14 C3
Trevanne Plat RH10 12 D6
Trevelyn Pl RH16 24 C4
Trewaren Ct RH11 11 E6
Treyford Cl RH11 10 C5
Triangle Rd RH16 26 D4
Triangle Way RH15 28 A6
Trinity Cl RH10 12 D6
Trinity Ct, Hassocks BN6 31 F6
Trinity Ct,
 Horsham RH12 34 C5
Trinity Rd BN6 31 E6
Troon Cl RH11 10 A5
Trotton Cl RH10 16 C2
Troymede RH17 17 C6
Trundle Mead RH12 34 C6
Tudor Cl, Crawley RH10 12 D6
Tudor Cl,
 East Grinstead RH19 21 E5
Tudor Gdns RH15 28 D6
Tulip Ct RH12 34 C5
Tullett Rd RH10 16 C2
Tunnmeade*,
 Fairway RH11 14 A1

Name	Ref
urkey La RH15	29 E4
urner Ct RH19	21 F2
urner Walk RH10	16 A3
urners Hill Rd, Crawley RH10	13 E5
urners Hill Rd, Crawley Down RH10	18 A3
urners Hill Rd, East Grinstead RH19	20 A4
urners Mill Cl RH16	24 B4
urners Mill Rd RH16	24 B4
urners Way RH15	28 C2
urnpike Pl RH11	11 G3
urret Cl*, Buckhurst Way RH19	20 B2
uscany Gdns RH10	11 G3
ushmore Av RH10	11 G2
ushmore Cres RH10	11 G3
ushmore Ct RH10	11 G3
ushmore La RH10	11 G3
ussock Cl RH11	14 D1
uxford Cl RH10	16 C1
veed La RH15	10 C3
witten La RH19	19 F2
wo Mile Ash RH13	36 A5
vyhurst Cl RH19	20 C2
vyne Cl RH11	14 C2
vyner Cl RH6	5 F3
ylden Way RH12	35 F3
yler Rd RH10	15 G2
ylers Grn RH17	23 D5
ymperley Ct RH13	35 E6
yne Cl RH10	16 D1
nderhill La BN6	32 A5
nderwood Cl RH10	18 D5
ofield RH6	4 D5
ofield Cl RH6	4 D6
opark Gdns RH12	35 F3
oper Beacon Rd BN6	33 F6
oper Forecourt RH6	8 C2
oper St Johns Rd RH15	28 D3
oper Stables RH16	26 A1
ale Dr RH12	36 C1
le Rd RH16	26 C3
lebridge Cl RH15	29 F1
lebridge Dr RH15	29 F1
lebridge Rd RH15	29 F2
lentine Dr RH15	28 B3
nbrugh Cl RH11	14 B2
ncouver Dr RH11	11 G2
nners RH10	11 G4
rbania Way RH19	21 F3
rnon Cl RH12	35 F5
carage La RH6	4 C3
carage Rd RH10	18 B6
ctoria Av RH15	28 B4
ctoria Cl, urgess Hill RH15	28 C4
ctoria Cl, Horley RH6	4 D4
ctoria Cl RH13	37 E2
ctoria Gdns RH15	28 B4
ctoria Ind Est, urgess Hill RH15	28 A4
ctoria Ind Est, urgess Hill RH15	28 C5
ctoria Rd, alcombe RH17	17 C5
ctoria Rd, urgess Hill RH15	28 B4
rawley RH11	3 A2
ctoria Rd, aywards Heath RH16	27 E1
ctoria Rd, Horley RH6	4 D4
ctoria St RH13	37 E2
ctoria Way, urgess Hill RH15	21 E6
ctoria Way, ast Grinstead RH19	21 E6
tory Rd RH12	34 B6
ws Path RH16	27 F1
all Gdns RH12	38 B1
cent Cl RH13	37 F2
ienne Cl RH11	11 G2
can Cl RH11	15 F3
ddington Cl RH11	14 D2
dham Cl RH10	12 C2
gg Cl RH19	21 E4
gtail Cl RH12	34 C2

Name	Ref
Wain End RH12	34 D4
Wainwrights RH11	15 F2
Wakehams Grn Dr RH10	13 E2
Wakehurst Dr RH10	15 F2
Wakehurst Mews RH12	36 A2
Waldby Ct*, Nevile Cl RH11	14 D2
Walesbeech RH10	12 B6
Walker Rd RH10	16 C1
Wall Hill Rd RH19	22 C3
Wallis Way, Burgess Hill RH15	28 B2
Wallis Way, Horsham RH13	35 G5
Walnut Cl RH13	37 F2
Walnut La RH11	11 E2
Walnut Pk RH16	27 F1
Waltersville Way RH6	5 F6
Walton Dr RH13	35 H5
Walton Heath RH10	13 E3
Wandle Cl RH10	16 C1
Wantage Cl RH10	16 C2
Warburton Cl RH11	21 F4
Warden Cl RH17	23 C4
Ware Ct RH15	29 G3
Warelands RH15	28 C5
Warner Cl RH10	16 C3
Warner Cl RH15	28 D4
Warnham Rd, Broadbridge Heath RH12	38 B2
Warnham Rd, Crawley RH10	16 B2
Warnham Rd, Horsham RH12	34 B4
Warren Cl RH19	19 G2
Warren Dr RH10	10 D4
Warrington Cl RH11	14 B3
Washington Rd, Crawley RH11	14 B3
Washington Rd, Haywards Heath RH16	25 E5
Wassand Cl RH15	12 B5
Water Lea RH10	16 B1
Water Vw*, Grays Wood RH6	5 F4
Watercress RH13	35 F6
Waterfield Dr RH13	37 F1
Waterfield Gdns RH11	14 B1
Waterside, East Grinstead RH19	21 F4
Waterside, Horley RH6	4 D2
Waterside Cl RH11	14 B1
Watson Cl RH10	16 C2
Waveney Walk*, Norwich Rd RH10	16 B1
Waverley Ct RH12	36 C1
Wayside RH11	14 B1
Weald Cl, Hassocks BN6	30 D2
Weald Cl, Horsham RH13	37 E3
Weald Dr RH10	12 A6
Weald Rd RH15	28 B3
Weald Rise RH16	26 D4
Wealden Way RH16	24 B6
Weaver Cl RH11	14 B1
Weavers Cl RH15	29 G5
Webb Cl RH11	15 E4
Weddell Rd RH10	15 H2
Weirbrook RH10	16 A2
Welbeck Cl RH15	29 G2
Welbeck Dr RH15	29 G2
Wellcroft Cotts BN6	30 A3
Weller Cl RH10	13 E6
Wellfield RH19	22 A1
Wellington Cl RH10	13 E2
Wellington Rd RH12	37 E1
Wellington Town Rd RH19	20 C2
Wellington Way RH6	4 C2
Wells Cl RH12	36 A1
Wells Lea RH19	20 C1
Wells Mdw RH19	20 C1
Wellwood Cl RH12	35 G5
Welwyn Cl RH11	14 B3
Wenlock Cl RH11	14 D1
Wensleydale RH11	15 F2
Wentworth Dr RH10	12 D4
Wesley Cl, Crawley RH11	14 B2
Wesley Cl, Horley RH6	4 D2
West Av RH10	12 A4

Name	Ref
West Common RH16	24 D4
West Common Dr RH16	25 E4
West Furlong Ct BN6	31 E3
West Furlong La BN6	31 E3
West Green Dr RH11	3 A1
West Hill RH19	20 C5
West Hill Dr RH15	28 C4
West Hill Walk RH15	28 C4
West La RH19	20 C5
West Leigh RH19	20 D5
West Mallions RH16	27 E2
West Par RH12	34 C5
West Park Cres RH15	28 B3
West Park Rd RH10	18 A2
West St, Burgess Hill RH15	28 B3
West St, Crawley RH11	3 B3
West St, East Grinstead RH19	20 D4
West St, Hassocks BN6	33 F3
West St, Horsham RH12	36 C1
West View Cotts RH16	25 F4
West View Gdns RH19	20 D4
West View Rd RH16	25 F4
West Way RH10	12 A5
Westcott Cl RH11	15 F5
Westcott Keep*, Langshott La RH6	5 E3
Western Rd, Burgess Hill RH15	28 C3
Western Rd, Hassocks BN6	30 D2
Western Rd, Haywards Heath RH16	26 D1
Westfield Rd RH11	11 E6
Westlands Rd RH16	25 F5
Westleas RH6	4 B2
Westminster Rd RH10	12 C6
Westons Cl RH12	34 D2
Westup Rd RH17	17 A5
Westway, Crawley RH10	9 G6
Westway, Horley RH6	8 C2
Wheatfield Way RH6	5 E2
Wheatsheaf Cl, Burgess Hill RH15	28 B2
Wheatsheaf Cl, Horsham RH13	35 E4
Wheatsheaf La RH17	23 C3
Wheatstone Cl RH10	8 B6
Wheeler Rd RH10	16 C1
Wheelers Way RH19	19 F2
Wheelwright La RH15	29 G5
Whistler Cl RH10	16 A2
White Hart Ct RH12	34 C5
White Horse Rd RH12	35 G3
Whitecroft RH6	5 E3
Whitehall Dr RH11	10 B6
Whitemans Cl RH17	23 B1
Whitemans Grn RH17	23 B2
Whites Cl RH11	31 E2
Whitgift Walk RH10	15 G2
Whitmore Way RH6	4 B3
Whittington Rd RH10	15 G2
Whittle Way RH10	8 B5
Whitworth Rd RH11	11 G1
Wickham Cl, Haywards Heath RH16	24 C4
Wickham Cl, Horley RH6	4 C3
Wickham Dr BN6	31 G4
Wickham Hill BN6	31 F4
Wickham Way RH16	24 C3
Wickhurst Gdns RH12	38 C2
Wickhurst La RH12	38 C2
Wickland Ct RH10	15 G2
Widgeon Way RH12	34 C4
Wilberforce Cl RH11	15 E5
Wilderness Rd BN6	31 E2
Wildgoose Dr RH12	38 D2
Wildwood RH12	38 D3
Wilkinson Ct RH11	15 E4
William Allen La RH16	25 F5
William Morris Way RH11	15 E5
Williams Way RH10	12 B5
Willow Brean RH6	4 B3
Willow Cl, Crawley RH11	11 H3
Willow Cl, East Grinstead RH19	20 B4
Willow Cl, Hassocks BN6	31 E2
Willow Corner RH6	6 C2
Willow Gdns BN6	31 E1
Willow Mead RH15	21 E5

Name	Ref
Willow Pk RH16	25 F6
Willow Rd RH12	35 G4
Willow Way BN6	31 E1
Willowfield RH11	3 B4
Willowrook Way BN6	32 C3
Wilmington Cl, Crawley RH11	15 E5
Wilmington Cl, Hassocks BN6	32 C2
Wilmington Way RH16	25 E5
Wilson Cl RH10	16 D2
Wilton Villas RH17	17 D5
Wimblehurst Rd RH12	34 C5
Wincanton Cl RH10	13 E5
Winchester Rd RH10	15 G3
Windermere Rd RH16	24 D6
Windmill Av BN6	32 C3
Windmill Cl, Horley RH6	5 E4
Windmill Cl, Horsham RH13	35 F6
Windmill Cl RH15	11 G3
Windmill Dr RH15	29 E3
Windmill La, Ashurst Wood RH19	22 A2
Windmill La, East Grinstead RH19	20 C1
Windrum Ct RH12	36 A3
Windrush Cl RH11	14 C1
Windsor Cl, Crawley RH11	15 F3
Windsor Cl, Haywards Heath RH16	26 C2
Windsor Pl RH19	21 E5
Windy Ridge RH11	10 D6
Wingle Tye Rd RH15	28 C5
Winkfield Ct RH16	24 C5
Winkhurst Way RH15	29 G6
Winnals Pk RH16	24 B5
Winners Way RH6	7 F2
Winterbourne RH12	35 F2
Winterfold RH10	16 A2
Winterton Ct RH13	37 E1
Wisborough Ct*, Cowfold RH15	14 C1
Wisden Av RH15	28 C2
Wiston Ct RH11	14 C2
Wither Dale RH6	4 B2
Withey Brook RH6	4 B6
Withey Mdws RH6	4 A6
Withy Bush RH15	28 B2
Wivelsfield Rd RH16	26 D2
Woburn Rd RH11	14 D1
Wold Cl RH11	14 C1
Woldhurstlea Cl RH11	14 D1
Wolstonbury Cl, Crawley RH11	15 F1
Wolstonbury Cl, Hassocks BN6	31 F4
Wolstonbury Ct RH15	29 E4
Wolstonbury Way RH15	29 E4
Wolverton Cl RH6	4 C6
Wolverton Gdns RH6	4 C5
Wood End RH12	35 H4
Wood Ride RH16	26 C2
Wood St RH19	20 C4
Woodbridge Ct RH12	35 F5
Woodbury Av RH19	21 F3
Woodbury Ct RH19	21 F5
Woodcote RH6	5 E3
Woodcourt RH11	15 F4
Woodcrest Rd RH15	28 D6
Woodcroft RH15	28 D2
Woodcroft Rd RH11	14 A1
Woodend RH10	12 B3
Woodfield Cl RH10	11 H4
Woodfield Rd RH10	3 E1
Woodgates Cl RH13	37 F1
Woodhall Cl RH17	23 B2
Woodhayes RH6	5 E3
Wooding Gro RH10	15 E5
Woodland Av RH15	29 F3
Woodland Cl, Burgess Hill RH15	29 F3
Woodland Cl, Horsham RH13	35 G5
Woodland Cres RH15	29 F3
Woodland Dr RH10	18 D6
Woodland Way RH15	35 G5
Woodlands, Crawley RH10	12 D3
Woodlands, Horley RH6	5 F3
Woodlands Cl RH10	18 D6
Woodlands Rd, East Grinstead RH19	21 E1

Name	Ref
Woodlands Rd, Haywards Heath RH16	24 D6
Woodleigh Rd RH15	29 F2
Woodmans Hill RH15	15 F4
Woodpecker Cres RH15	28 A4
Woodridge Cl RH10	27 E1
Woodroyd Av RH6	4 C5
Woodroyd Gdns RH6	4 C5
Woods Hill Cl RH19	22 B2
Woods Hill La RH19	22 B2
Woodside RH13	35 G6
Woodside Rd RH10	12 A3
Woodsland Cl BN6	32 B2
Woodsland Rd BN6	32 B2
Woodstock RH10	20 B3
Woodstock Cl RH12	34 B4
Woodwards RH11	15 E4
Woodwards Cl RH15	29 F6
Woolborough Rd RH10	11 G4
Woolborough La RH10	11 G3
Woolborough Rd RH10	18 C6
Woolven Cl RH15	28 C6
Worcester Rd RH10	15 H3
Wordsworth Cl RH10	12 C4
Wordsworth Pl RH12	35 E2
Wordsworth Rise RH19	20 B4
Worsted La RH19	21 G5
Worth Ct RH10	12 D5
Worth Park Av RH10	12 C4
Worth Way RH10	12 C5
Worthing Rd RH12	13 E6
Wray Cl RH19	22 B2
Wren Cl, Burgess Hill RH15	28 A4
Wren Cl, Horsham RH12	34 D2
Wren Ct RH10	15 H2
Wright Cl RH10	16 C4
Wroxham Walk*, Norwich Rd RH10	16 B1
Wyberlye Rd RH15	28 D3
Wychperry Rd RH16	24 B5
Wycliffe Ct*, Booth Rd RH11	14 B3
Wye Cl RH11	15 F5
Wykeham Way RH15	29 F5
Wynlea Cl RH10	18 B6
Wysemead RH6	5 F3
Wythwood RH16	26 D3
Yale Dr RH12	34 B6
Yarmouth Cl RH10	16 B1
Yarrow Cl RH12	34 D4
Yattendon Rd RH6	5 E4
Yew La RH19	20 A2
Yew Tree Cl RH6	4 D3
Yew Tree Ct RH17	23 C3
Yew Tree Rd RH6	6 B2
Yewlands Walk*, Fairway RH11	14 A1
York Av RH19	21 E5
York Cl RH13	35 F6
York Rd, Burgess Hill RH15	28 B4
York Rd, Crawley RH10	15 H3

For an up-to-date publication list and latest prices visit our web site at

www.estate-publications.co.uk

Use the search facility to find the village, town or city you require.

Local Red Books (selection of)

Ashford & Tenterden	Lancaster & Morecambe
Barnstaple & Ilfracombe	Lincoln
Basildon & Billericay	Macclesfield & Wilmslow
Basingstoke & Andover	Maidstone
Bath & Bradford-upon-Avon	Medway & Gillingham
Bedford	Newport & Chepstow
Brentwood	Northampton
Bromley (London Borough)	Norwich
Burton-upon-Trent & Swadlincote	Nuneaton & Bedworth
Cambridge	Oxford & Abingdon
Chelmsford, Braintree & Maldon	Peterborough
Chester	Plymouth, Saltash & Torpoint
Chesterfield	Reading & Henley-on-Thames
Chichester & Bognor Regis	Redditch & Bromsgrove
Colchester & Clacton	Rugby
Crewe	Salisbury, Amesbury & Wilton
Eastbourne, Bexhill, Seaford & Newhaven	Sevenoaks
Exeter & Exmouth	Southend-on-Sea
Fareham & Gosport	Stafford
Folkestone, Dover, Deal & Romney Marsh	Swindon
Gloucester & Cheltenham	Telford
Gravesend & Dartford	Tunbridge Wells & Tonbridge
Great Yarmouth & Lowestoft	Warwick & Royal Leamington Spa
Hereford	Weston-super-Mare & Clevedon
Ipswich & Felixstowe	Winchester
Kidderminster	Wolverhampton (Sheet Map)
Kingston-upon-Hull	York

Super Red Books

Birmingham (Colour)
Bournemouth
Brighton
Bristol
Cardiff
Coventry
Derby
Edinburgh
Glasgow
Leicester
Nottingham
Portsmouth
Southampton (Colour)
Stoke-on-Trent
Swansea

County Red Books

Bedfordshire	Lincolnshire
Berkshire	Norfolk
Buckinghamshire	Northamptonshire
Cambridgeshire	Nottinghamshire
Cheshire	Oxfordshire
Cornwall	Shropshire
Derbyshire	Somerset
Devon	Staffordshire
Dorset	Suffolk
Essex	Surrey
Gloucestershire	Sussex (East)
Hampshire	Sussex (West)
Herefordshire	Warwickshire
Kent	Wiltshire
Leicestershire & Rutland	Worcestershire

Estate Publications, Bridewell House, Tenterden, Kent, TN30 6EP
Tel: 01580 764225   Fax: 01580 763720